ANDREW MARTIN

Interior Design Review Volume 20

teNeues

The 20 years of the Andrew Martin Interior Designer of the Year Award have documented and chronicled the design world's narrative since 1996. We have been proud to showcase the work of hundreds of designers from every corner of the globe. These designers have articulated the zeitgeist of the moment. Kelly Hoppen, our inaugural winner, for 20 years has defined not just a look but a whole approach to life. Stephen Falcke encapsulated the creativity of Africa in the afterglow of Mandela's release from Robben Island. The late great Alberto Pinto was the greatest French designer of his generation and the quintessential designers' designer. Kit Kemp re-imagined the way hotels could be.

Zeynep Fadillioglu smashed through the prejudice of centuries to become the first woman to design a mosque. Axel Vervoordt's ground breaking exhibition at the Louvre is still talked about and his relaxed sophistication has shaped a whole generation. Martyn Lawrence – Bullard awakened the ghost of Hollywood glamour. Rose Uniacke proved that antiques could be hip. Nobody has done more to energise the powerhouse of Chinese design than Steve Leung.

Throughout all this time and indeed for 20 years before, Nicholas Ponsonby Haslam has been a legendary figure. He embodies the maxim, design is about personality. As befits the son of Queen Victoria's goddaughter, Nicky is friend of the famous (and lover to quite a few of them). His achievements betray his prodigious work rate. Cloaked like the Scarlet Pimpernel in a disguise of effortless ease, from cowboy to fashion icon, cabaret star and journalism regular, Nicky is probably the most loved designer on the planet. He is a happy and fitting pinnacle to mark the 20 years of the Andrew Martin Interior Designer of the Year Award.

Martin Waller

Nicky Haslam

Designer: Nicky Haslam. Company: Nicky Haslam Studio, London, UK. Forty years of creating highly individual and exquisitely finished projects, concentrating on private clients, many of them celebrities. Currently finalising the design of a renowned house in Newmarket and restoring an 18th Century classical mansion, a dining pavilion on the Isle of Wight and the renovation of a tiny cottage in a Hampshire hamlet. Recently completed a townhouse in New Orleans, an apartment in Manhattan's Time-Warner building and a new build in Surrey. Design philosophy: all buildings have voices. Listening is the most important thing. Comfort, pleasure, manageability.

Vincent Van Duyse

Designer: Vincent Van Duysen. Company: Vincent Van Duysen Architects, Antwerp, Belgium. An architectural office with a strong sense for interior and product design. Projects include residential, commercial and hotels, for clients in Belgium as well as in the rest of the world. Recent work includes the Alexander Wang flagship store in London, a boat project in the US, the interior of an office building in Beirut and a furniture collection for Molteni&C. Current projects include apartments in Paris, residences in Belgium as well as in LA and Southampton, a hotel and senior residence in Antwerp, product design for Flos and B&B Italia and the creative directory for Molteni&C. Design philosophy: pared-down aesthetic, where functionality, durability and comfort are prime components; using pure and tactile materials to create a clear and timeless design.

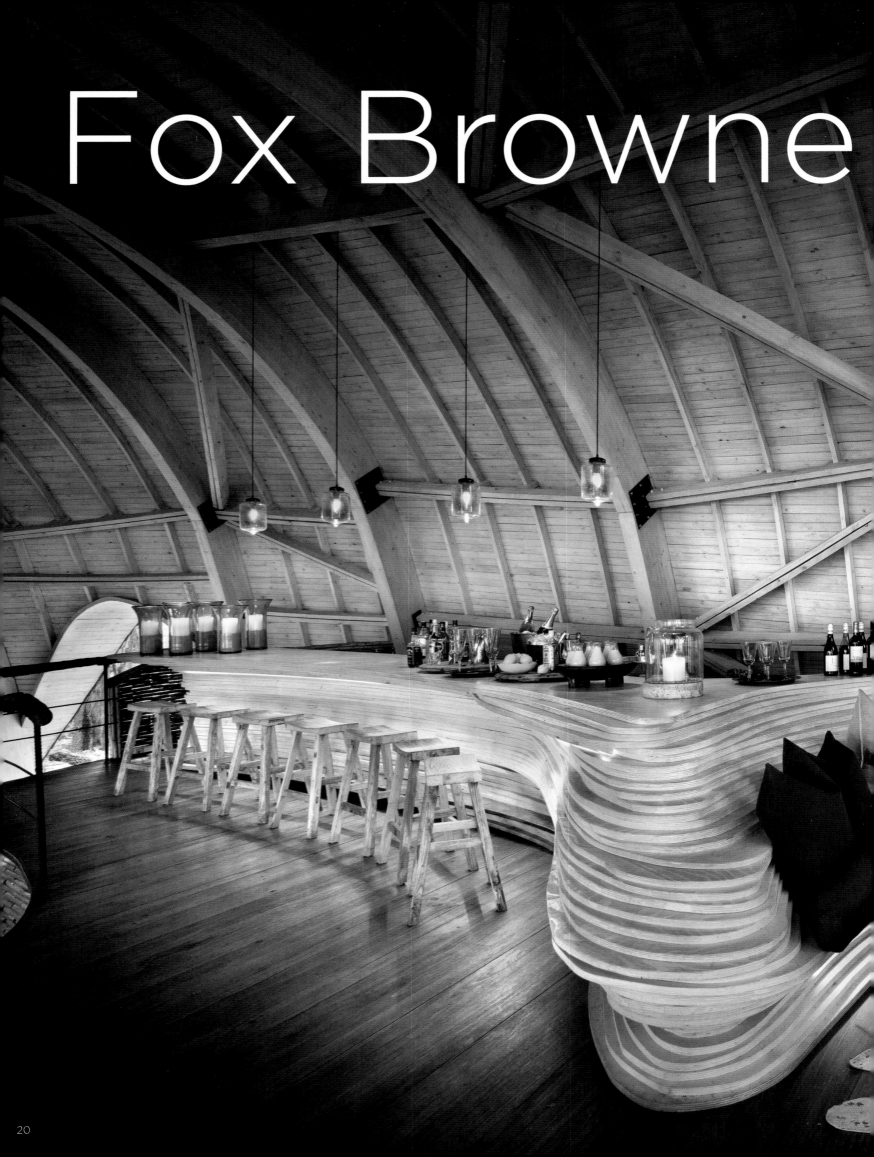

Fox Browne

Creative

Designers: Chris Browne & Debra Fox. Fox Browne Creative, Johannesburg, South Africa. Specialising in creative, elegant, cost effective and sustainable solutions, in the luxury sector of the hospitality and retail industry. Recent work includes Sandibe Okavango safari lodge, a luxury camp in Botswana, Mabote House, Waterberg, a private bush home in South Africa and Somalisa camp, Hwange National Park, a luxury tented safari lodge in Zimbabwe. Current projects include Nxabega Okavango, tented camp, Belhambra estate, a residential development in Johannesburg and Sirai beach house, a private villa in Kilifi, Kenya. Design philosophy: merge beautiful spaces with gracious hospitality for the luxury international traveller.

Cindy Rinfret

Designer: Cindy Rinfret. Company: Rinfret, Ltd. Interior Design & Decoration, Greenwich, CT, USA. Specialising in luxury interior design and decoration in Connecticut, New York City and across the United States including both primary and secondary private homes for high profile and celebrity clients. Recent work includes a home in Greenwich, an expansive Jacobean style new build and Tommy Hilfiger's waterfront penthouse duplex at the iconic Plaza Hotel in New York City. Current projects include an eclectic home in Westport, CT, a beautiful family home in Greenwich, CT. and Tommy Hilfiger's historic Tudor home in Greenwich, CT. Design philosophy: comfortable, luxurious, understated.

Ching-Ping Chang

Designer: Ching-Ping Chang. Company: Tienfun Interior Planning, Taiwan. Predominantly luxury, residential developments and boutique hotels in greater China and overseas. Current work includes One restaurant inside a hotel in Tainan, Taiwan, the lobby of a residential building in Shenzhen and a boutique store in Taichung, Taiwan. Design philosophy: new oriental montage.

Kim Stephen

Designer: Kim Stephen. Company: Kim Stephen Interiors, London, UK. Specialising in residential and hospitality interiors from Cape Town to London. Current projects include a substantial beach home in Plettenberg Bay, South Africa, a luxury seaside apartment in Cape Town, a family home in South West London and an apartment in South Kensington. Recent projects include large, residential homes on both sides of Table Mountain in Cape Town, a villa in St Tropez and an apartment in London. Design philosophy: playful, vibrant, relaxed, liveable.

Stephen Ryan

Designer: Stephen Ryan. Company: Stephen Ryan Design & Decoration, London, UK. Luxury residential, corporate and boutique hotels internationally. Recent projects include a villa in Oman, a country house in Norfolk and a penthouse in London. Current work includes an apartment & townhouse in London and a penthouse in Malta. Design philosophy: quality, symmetry, colour, drama, wit.

Aleksandra Laska

Designer: Aleksandra Laska. Company: Ola Laska, Warsaw, Poland. Specialising in individual interiors. Recent projects include the partial remodelling of 1,700 sq. m. of the National Opera House in Warsaw, an artist's studio and theatre space design within an old factory. Current work includes Karolina Wajda's Andalusian Lustiano Horse Riding Academy. Design philosophy: to confront the present with the past.

Figur. 36   *3 part*

M. de Plu.

Erin Martin

Designer: Erin Martin. Company: Erin Martin Design, California, USA. Recent projects include Trinchero Family Estates Winery, Napa Valley, a private residence in Martis Camp, CA and a tasting room in Napa. Current work includes a private residence in Beverly Hills, Four Seasons in Napa Valley and Bottlerock Headquarters, also in Napa. Design philosophy: it's never done – survive and have plastic surgery.

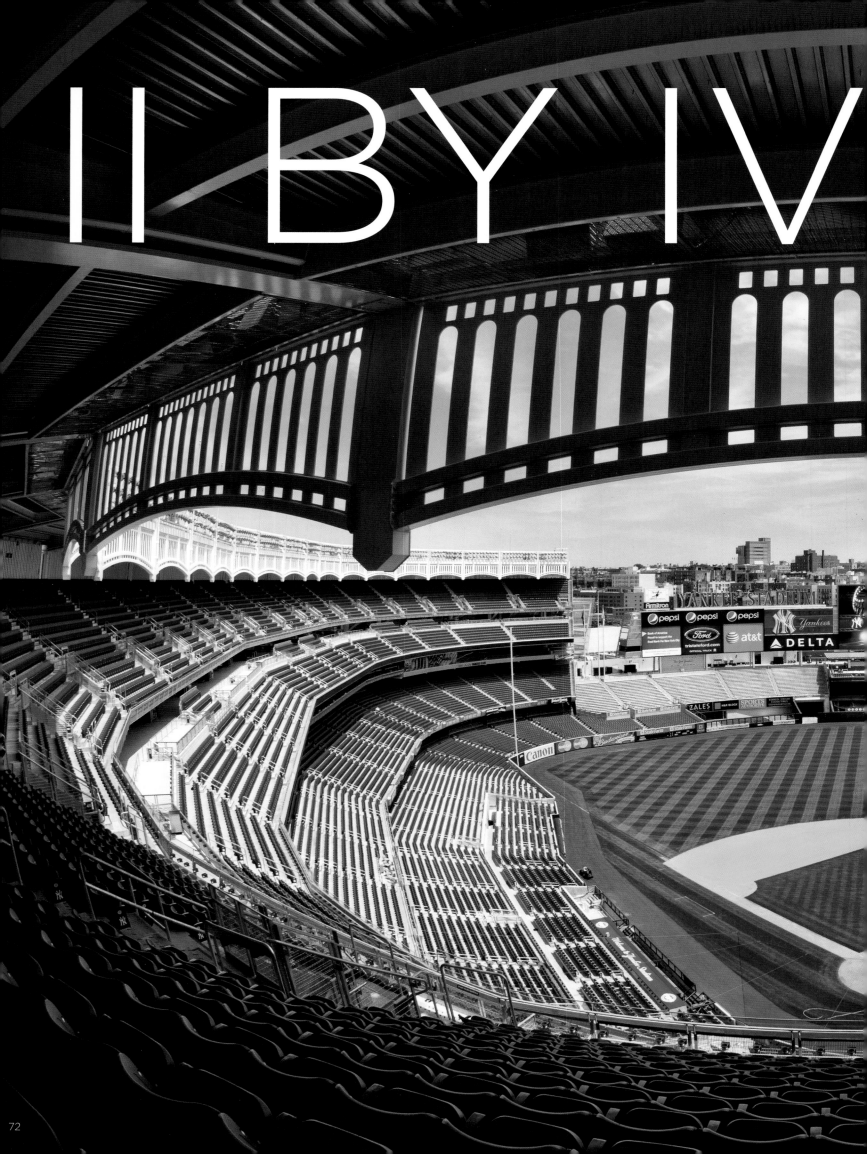

II BY IV

Design

Designers: Dan Menchions & Keith Rushbrook. Company: II BY IV DESIGN, Toronto, Canada. A multi disciplinary studio with a focus on product design, retail spaces, hospitality environments, marine design, high end condominium developments and commercial offices. Current projects include the refurbishment of an Austrian river boat, a master planned waterfront community in San Francisco and the roll out of a UK based franchise in Canada. Recent works include a five star, international hotel in Toronto, as well as a Japanese restaurant and boutique lifestyle condominium also in Toronto. Design philosophy: passionate in realising the client's unique vision.

LSD Casa

Designer: Kot Ge. Company: LSD CASA. Established in 2007, specialising in premium custom design to real estate developers and individuals, including hotels, businesses, clubs, villas and show apartments. Recent projects include two CIFI Park Mansion Villas, Shanghai and Shui On Land gallery. Design philosophy: beyond the tide.

Jan Showers

Designer: Jan Showers. Company: Jan Showers & Associates, Dallas, Texas, USA. Listed by Architectural Digest in the world's top 100 designers, Showers also has an antique showroom in Dallas as well as a high end furniture line sold in eight showrooms across the U.S. Recent projects include a compound in Paradise Valley, Scottsdale, AZ, a townhouse in Belgravia, London and a residential home in Highland Park, Dallas. Current work includes a second home in Hawaii, a high rise apartment in New York City, a ranch in the Texas Hill Country and a second home in Nantucket, MA. Design philosophy: to create a work of art that fulfils the client's needs and desires.

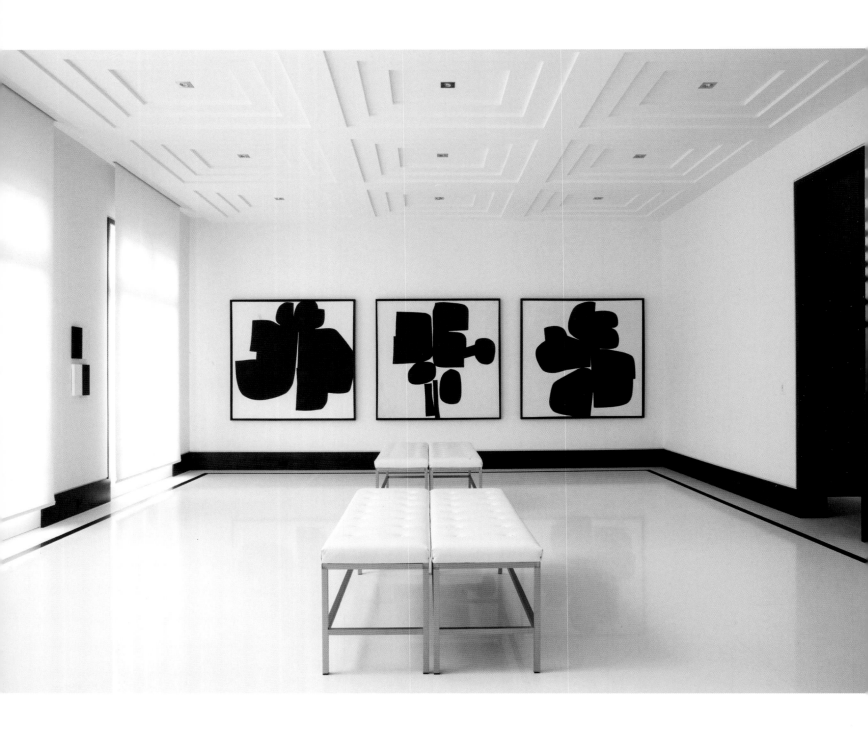

Stefano Dorata

Designer: Stefano Dorata. Company: Studio Dorata, Rome, Italy. Offices, apartments, villas, yachts and hotels, throughout Europe, America and Asia. Current projects include a villa in Lugano, a rural house in Montalcino and a house in London. Recent work includes a villa in Florence, a rural house in Rome and a villa in Bali. Design philosophy: simplicity and order.

Cui Shu

Designer: Cui Shu. Company: New Look Design Co. Ltd, Beijing, China. An award winning team who develop intimate spaces that resonate. Current projects include Third District Club, Rosemoo office and Anaya prototype space. Recent projects include MOMA apartment, Fragrance Hill, Moyu mansions and a coffee shop. Design philosophy: intimacy in creation, to build a better lifestyle.

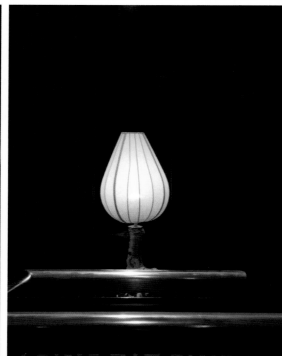

Jorge Cañete

Croyez ceux qui cherchent la vérité, doutez de ceux qui la trouvent.

André Gide, Ainsi soit-il ou Les Jeux sont faits

Designer: Jorge Cañete. Company: Interior Design Philosophy, Vaud, Switzerland. Work is predominantly residential, including a contemporary mansion facing the lake in Geneva and an old charterhouse. Recent projects have involved an art gallery in a 14th Century cloister, the creation of different collections of poetic artefacts and the beginnings of a new interior design book. Design philosophy: analyse the environment, the location and the client.

Gang Cao & Yanan Yan

Designer: Gang Cao & Yanan Yan. Company: Henan Erheyong Architectural Decoration Design, Henan Province, China. Specialising in design for commercial, residential and catering spaces. Recent projects include the office of Henan Zhengzhou Hua'an Property, Henan Zhengzhou 3D Printing Science Centre and Shanxi Taiyuan Pastry Store. Design philosophy: rational, emotional, perceptive, impressive.

Black & Spiro

Designer: Anna Spiro. Company: Black & Spiro Interior Design, Brisbane, Australia. Specialising in residential and commercial projects for prominent clients along the East coast of Australia. Current work includes a Victorian terraced house in Melbourne, the restoration of a large, iconic residence in the beach side town of Sorrento, Victoria and a grand Victorian home in one of Sydney's beautiful harbourside locations. Recent projects include a historic Queenslander located in the North of Brisbane, an inner city apartment in Brisbane and a beautiful country residence in one of New South Wales' most picturesque towns. Design philosophy: interesting, enduring, awe inspiring.

Toni Espuch

Designer: Toni Espuch. Company: AZULTIERRA, Barcelona, Spain. Luxury interior architecture worldwide. Current projects include a restaurant in Barcelona, a cottage in Southern Spain and a home in Barcelona. Recent work includes a hair salon, a pharmacy, a fair stand and residential houses around Spain. Design philosophy: search for beauty.

Tomoko Ikegai

Designer: Tomoko Ikegai. Company: ikg inc. Tokyo, Japan. Offering a wide range of architectural services, including façade, interior, lighting and landscape design as well as audio and security coordination, art and furniture selection. Recent projects include Tsutaya Electrics store in Tokyo, a unique 7,000 sq. m. lifestyle themed store blending civilization (electronics) and culture (books), a B&B Italia showroom in Tokyo and a seaside house with pool. Design philosophy: rich, uplifting, fascinating.

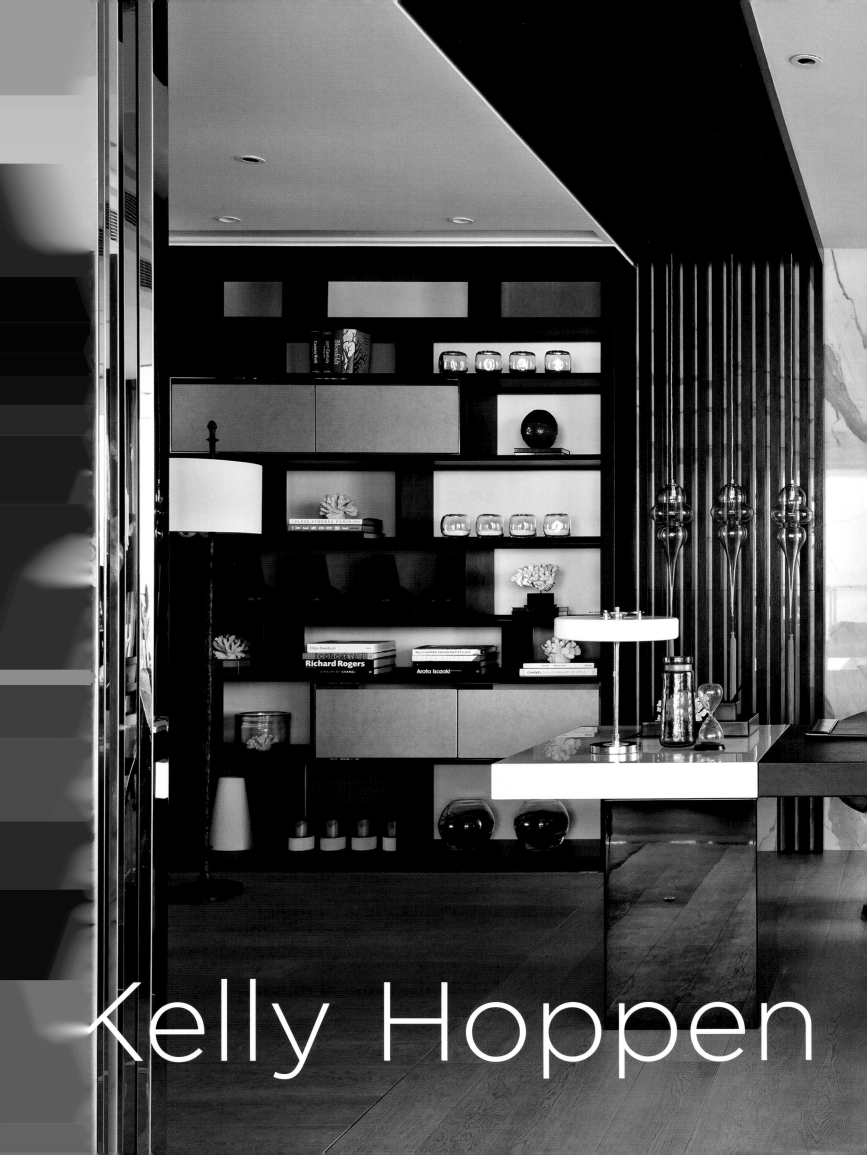

Kelly Hoppen

Designer: Kelly Hoppen. Company: Kelly Hoppen Interiors, London, UK. A globally renowned designer, entrepreneur, author and educator, Kelly's iconic, neutral style is featured in homes and commercial properties all over the world. She has received numerous awards and accolades throughout her career, including the inaugural Andrew Martin International Designer of the Year Award and an MBE for services to interior design. Recent projects include Da-An Towers in Taipei, private apartments in Kensington and apartments in Shenzhen and Shimao, China. Current work includes The Pearl 95 yacht, private homes in Hong Kong and villas in Pune, India. Design philosophy: to combine clean lines of the East with opulent textures from the West, to create elegant, dramatic and immaculate interiors.

Gisbert Pöppler

Designer: Gisbert Pöppler. Company: Gisbert Pöppler Architektur Interieur, Berlin, Germany. Luxury interior architecture and design both in Germany and internationally; with a strong focus on high end residential. Recent projects include a large renovated home in the German countryside, several private apartments throughout Berlin and an executive's London home. Current work ranges from a luxury 360° penthouse, a temporary fine furniture and art showcase in New York and a large country house in Germany. Design philosophy: traditional and modern in balance.

Fantastic Design Works

Designers: Katsunori Suzuki & Eiichi Maruyama. Company: Fantastic Design Works, Tokyo, Japan. Established in April 2001, specialising in interior, architectural, product and graphic design. Recent projects include Avion restaurant at Narita International Airport, Emiria wiz, an apparel store in Shinjuku, Tokyo and Ishigamaya Hamburg, a restaurant in Urawamisono, Japan. Current projects include Ishigamaya Hamburg & 3 Little Eggs in Yokohama, Igu & Peace restaurant in Himeji and Club R nightclub in Roppongi. Design philosophy: touching.

Zeynep Fadıllıoğlu

Designer: Zeynep Fadıllıoğlu. Company: Zeynep Fadıllıoğlu Design, Istanbul, Turkey. Specialising in luxury interior architecture in Europe, the Middle East and overseas, including both primary and secondary private homes, luxury residential developments and boutique hotels. Current projects include a resort in the Maldives, mansions in Oman, India and Jordan; a seaside restaurant & club in Turkey, a flat in London and major residential homes and executive offices in Istanbul. Recent work includes a shop in Geneva, beach houses in the South of Turkey and 'Yali' a Bosphorus mansion in Istanbul. Design philosophy: Ottoman, Eastern, Western, Universal.

Designers: Ajax Law & Virginia Lung. Company: One Plus Partnership Ltd. Hong Kong. Established in 2004, in 2012, One Plus were the first Asian winners of the Andrew Martin International Interior Designer of the Year Award. Recent work includes various cinema projects throughout China, a café in Shenzhen and several jewellery shops in China and Hong Kong. Design philosophy: bold, divergent, driven.

One Plus
Partnership

Hare + Klein

Designer: Meryl Hare. Company: Hare + Klein, Sydney, Australia. Predominantly residential interior design and hospitality, including boutique hotels and luxury yachts. Current projects include a heritage listed, country boutique hotel and substantial residences throughout Australia and the UK. Recent work includes a beach house in Bondi, a mansion on Sydney harbour and a major residence in Sydney. Design philosophy: original, creative, nurturing.

Enis Karavil

Designer: Enis Karavil. Sanayi 313 Architects, Istanbul, Turkey. Exclusive and bespoke design environments from Istanbul to New York, London to Saudi Arabia. Sanayi 313 combine design, art and food. Current projects include an apartment in Mercer Street, New York, a vineyard house in Bozcaada Island, Turkey and a residence at Zorlu Center, Istanbul. Recent work includes apartments in Notting Hill, London, Bosphorus Bebek, Istanbul and an historic mansion in Emirgan, Istanbul. Design philosophy: to combine modern attitude with traditional craftsmanship.

Roughan Interiors

Designer: Christina Sullivan Roughan. Company: Roughan Interiors, Weston CT & NYC, USA. Specialising in luxury interiors throughout the world, including primary and secondary homes, boutique projects, cruise liners, marina suites and hotels. Current projects include Stone Estate at the Greenbrier Sporting Club, West Virgina, a 5th Avenue historic townhouse, NYC and a New Canaan CT, Georgian estate. Recent work includes an historic captain's house, Nantucket MA, a waterfront estate in Greenwich, CT, a modern beach house in Los Angeles and a contemporary mountain house in Telluride, CO. Design philosophy: curated, purposeful, timeless, elegant.

Yu Ping

Designer: Yu Ping. Company: Xidian University, Shanxi Province, China. Specialising in boutique hotels, tea houses and private homes in China. Current projects include a hotel in the Guanzhong area of Shanxi Province in North China, Waku No. 17, the Seventeenth in the 'Waku' (tea tasting paradise) series, located in Zhengzhou and Waku No. 21 in Chengdu. Design philosophy: let the sunlight in and the air flow.

glenn Gissler

185

Designer: Glenn Gissler. Company: Glenn Gissler Design, New York, USA. A boutique practice specialising in new builds and renovations as well as the acquisition of fine and decorative arts. Current projects include a new, vernacular waterfront home in Maine, a Greek revival farmhouse & grounds in Litchfield County, Connecticut and an all wood resort on Shelter Island, the East End of Long Island. Recent work includes a large penthouse terrace for Michael Kors, a grand scale maisonette and a family townhouse, all in Greenwich Village, New York City. Design philosophy: the pursuit of design alchemy.

Geir Oterkjaer

Designer: Geir Oterkjaer. Company: Slettvoll Sthlm, Stockholm, Sweden. Predominantly private residences in Sweden, with some holiday homes in Spain and France. Recent projects include an old summerhouse in the South of Sweden, a compact flat in Stockholm city centre and a hotel lounge outside Stockholm. Current work includes a flower shop, a retro Caravan and an exclusive villa outside Stockholm. Design philosophy: listen to the character of the house.

Li Zurong & Bjoern

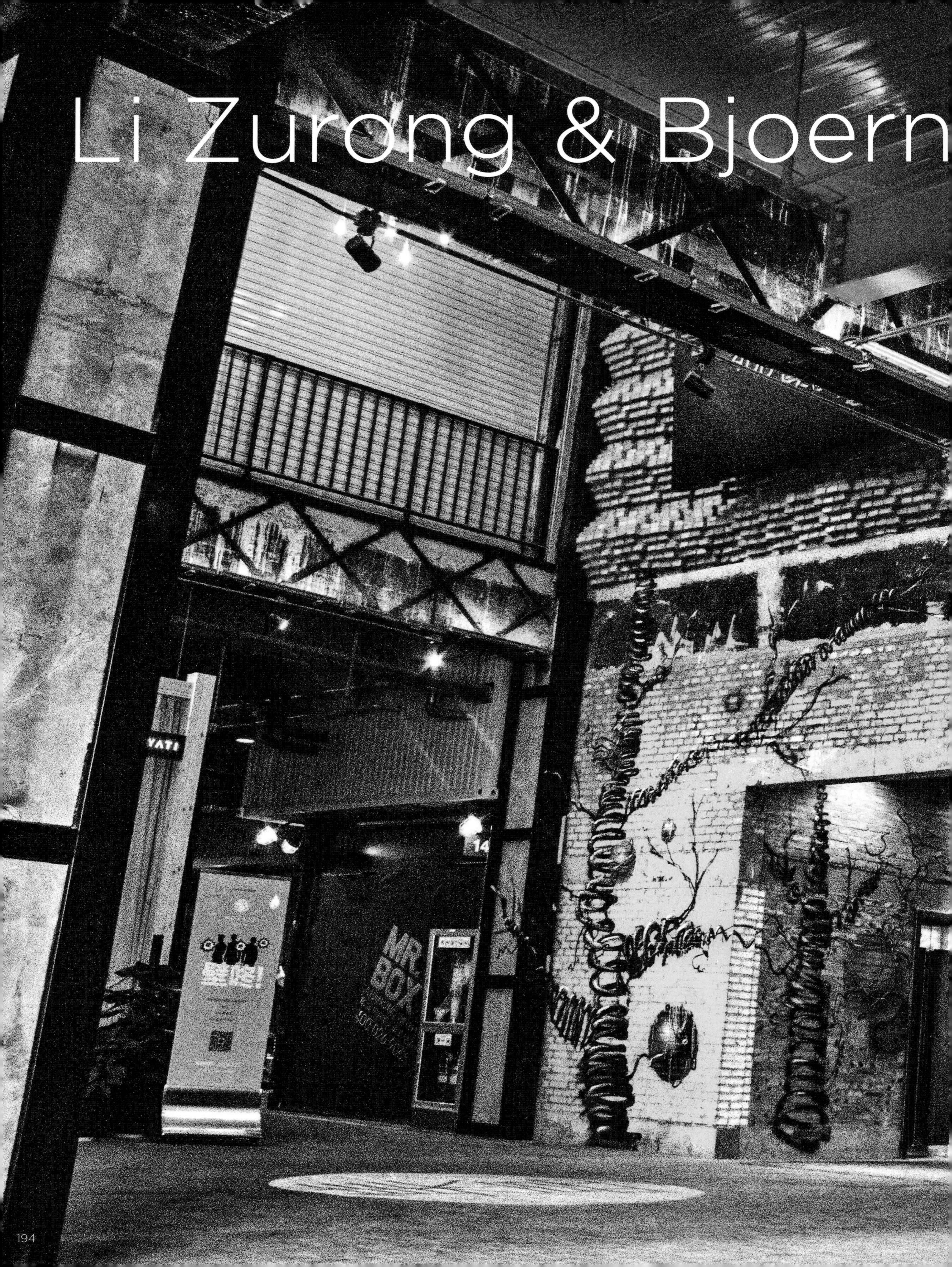

Rechtenbach

Designers: Li Zurong & Bjoern Rechtenbach. Company: Season Interior Design, Shanghai, China. Specialising in commercial interior design. Recent projects include MR.BOX, a business transformation project, in Ningbo, China; Shanghai Workers Cultural Palace rebuilt to create an industrial cluster, service life business; preparation of the Shanghai Wujiaochang project of 30,000 sq. m. of commercial buildings into a complex for young people to create a 'young country.' Design philosophy: creating cultural and commercial value.

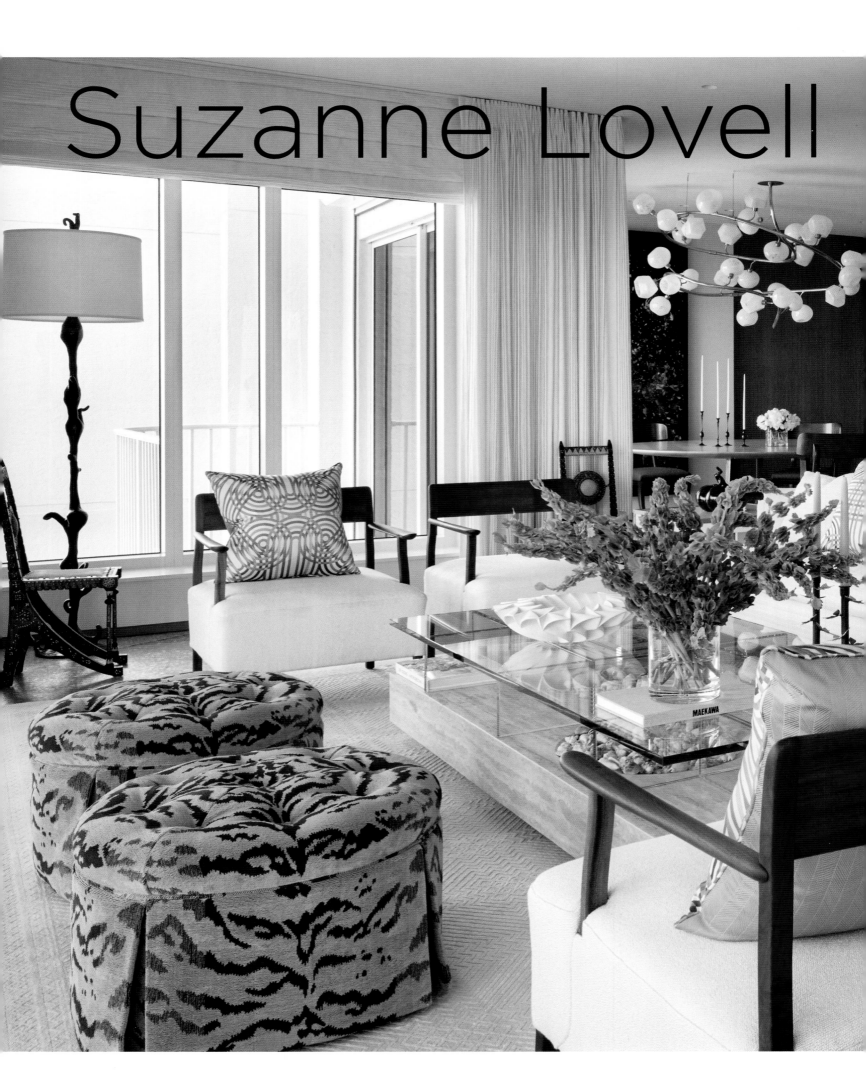

Designer: Suzanne Lovell. Company: Suzanne Lovell Inc., Chicago, USA. Work is international for private clients. Current work includes a beachfront compound in the Dominican Republic, a prominent penthouse in downtown Chicago, a significant Florida Gulf Coast residence and a large lake front family vacation home in Michigan. Recent work includes a Manhattan pied-à-terre, the full restoration of a landmarked Howard Van Doren Shaw co-op in Chicago, the renovation of an historic residence in Upstate New York and a contemporary, multi-unit penthouse in Miami Beach, Florida. Design philosophy: create couture environments for extraordinary living.

Coisas da

Terra

Designer: Rosarinho Gabriel. Company: Coisas da Terra – Arte e Decoração, Lda. Lisbon, Portugal. Work is international, with an emphasis on the renovation and decoration of private houses, hotels, restaurants, spas and offices. Recent examples include Torre de Palma Wine Hotel in Monforte, Portugal and a variety of private properties including a house in Penha Longa and an apartment in Cascais. Current work includes a hotel in Porto, two private houses in Cascais and Sintra as well as the transformation of a villa into a hotel in Colares. Design philosophy: free the imagination.

Evolution Design

Designers: Tianqi Guan, Lei Jin. Company: Evolution Design, Beijing, China. A team of over 30 professionals, specialising in boutique projects, from architectural planning and interior design to landscape and lighting design. Current work includes a hotel which sits on a Ko Samui cliff in Thailand, a boutique resort in Beijing Huairou district and a rural village renovation project in Beijing's Yanqing district. Recent projects include the restoration of a traditional courtyard house in Beijing Hutong, a cultural museum for Beijing Institute of Fashion Technology and a research laboratory for an internationally renowned fashion brand in the capital's University of Physical Education. Design philosophy: find the best solution, use authentic design.

Kim Scodro

Designer: Kim Scodro. Company: Kim Scodro Interiors, Chicago, USA. A boutique design studio based in Chicago and Phoenix. Current work includes a pre-war co-op in downtown Chicago, a mountain retreat in Flagstaff, Arizona and a show house room on the Upper East side in New York. Design philosophy: take inspiration from the client.

Ligia Casanova

Designer: Ligia Casanova. Company: Atelier Lígia Casanova, Lisbon, Portugal. Specialising in residential and public spaces. Current projects include a library/restaurant in Lisbon, a farmhouse in the North of Portugal and three beach houses in the South. Recent work includes a medical clinic in Lisbon, a private condominium of apartments in Northern Portugal and a luxury apartment in Lisbon. Design philosophy: to make room for happiness.

danse dans le vent
caresse l'air doucement
il fait si beau,
il fait si bon.

Lever les yeux au ciel
décrocher les étoiles

Pippa Paton

Designer: Pippa Paton. Company: Pippa Paton Design, Oxfordshire, UK. Complete interior design, architecture and project management solutions for high end primary and secondary residences across the Cotswolds, Home Counties and London. Recent projects include a Grade II listed Cotswold manor house, a 19th Century Cotswold barn with outbuildings and a London mews house. Current work includes a 10,000 sq.ft. North London townhouse, a large Oxfordshire estate and several cottages and barns throughout the Cotswolds. Design philosophy: functional, eclectic, curated.

Designer: Yasumichi Morita. Company: GLAMOROUS co.,ltd., Japan. Specialising in restaurants, bars, retail shops, offices, residences and hotels in Japan and overseas. Current projects include an Iron Chef's restaurant in Las Vegas and two department stores in Kuala Lumpur and Seoul. Recent work include Resona Bank, Tokyo, Kamishichiken Japanese hotel in Kyoto and Porcelain Nude photo collection, exhibited in Paris. Design philosophy: to provide "GLAMOROUS" design.

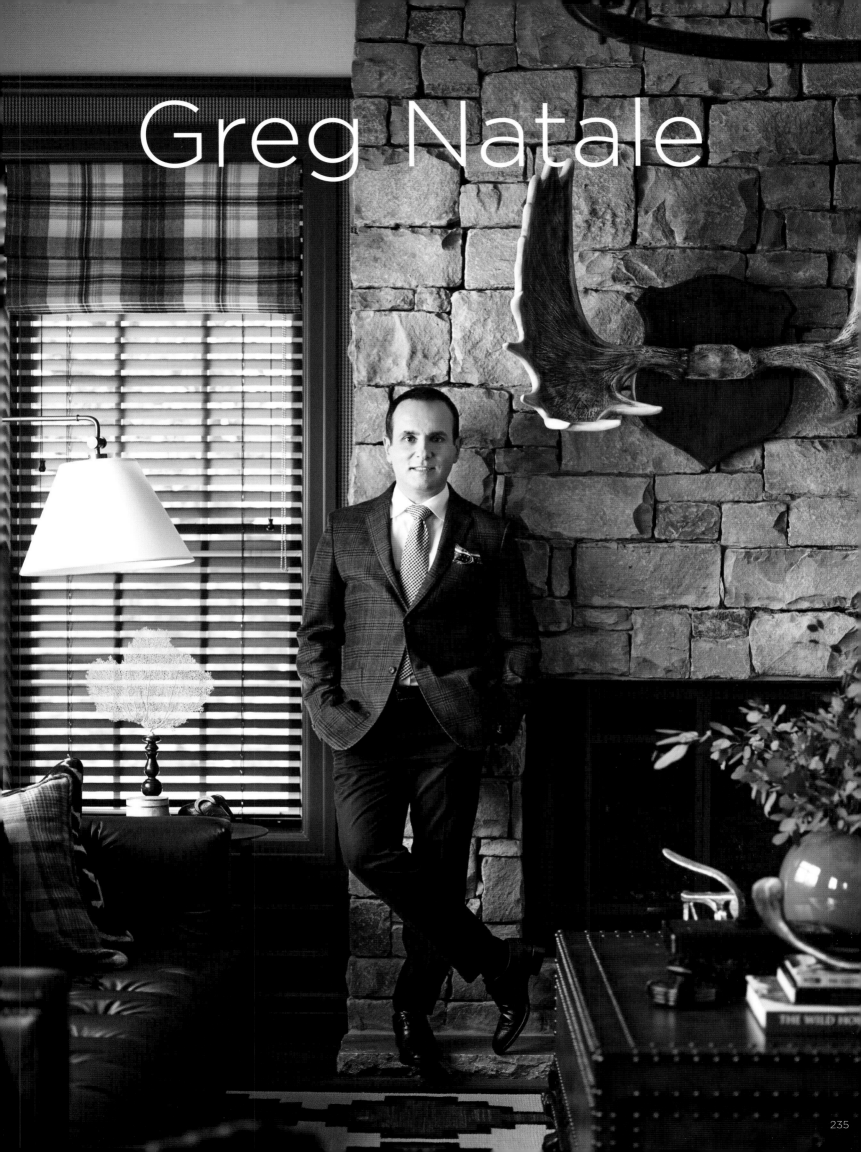

Greg Natale

Designer: Greg Natale. Company: Greg Natale Design, Sydney, Australia. Predominantly high end residential, luxurious retail and hospitality design, including signature collections of furniture and home ware designs sold in Australia and around the world. Current projects include a 100 room beachside luxury hotel in Perth, a decadent Hamptons inspired hilltop beach house in New South Wales and a ski chalet in New Zealand. Recent projects include a luxury hotel in the Hunter Valley wine region of Australia, a signature range of bed linen and towels as well as a marble mosaic tile collection. Design philosophy: bold, recognisable, sought after.

Katharine

Pooley

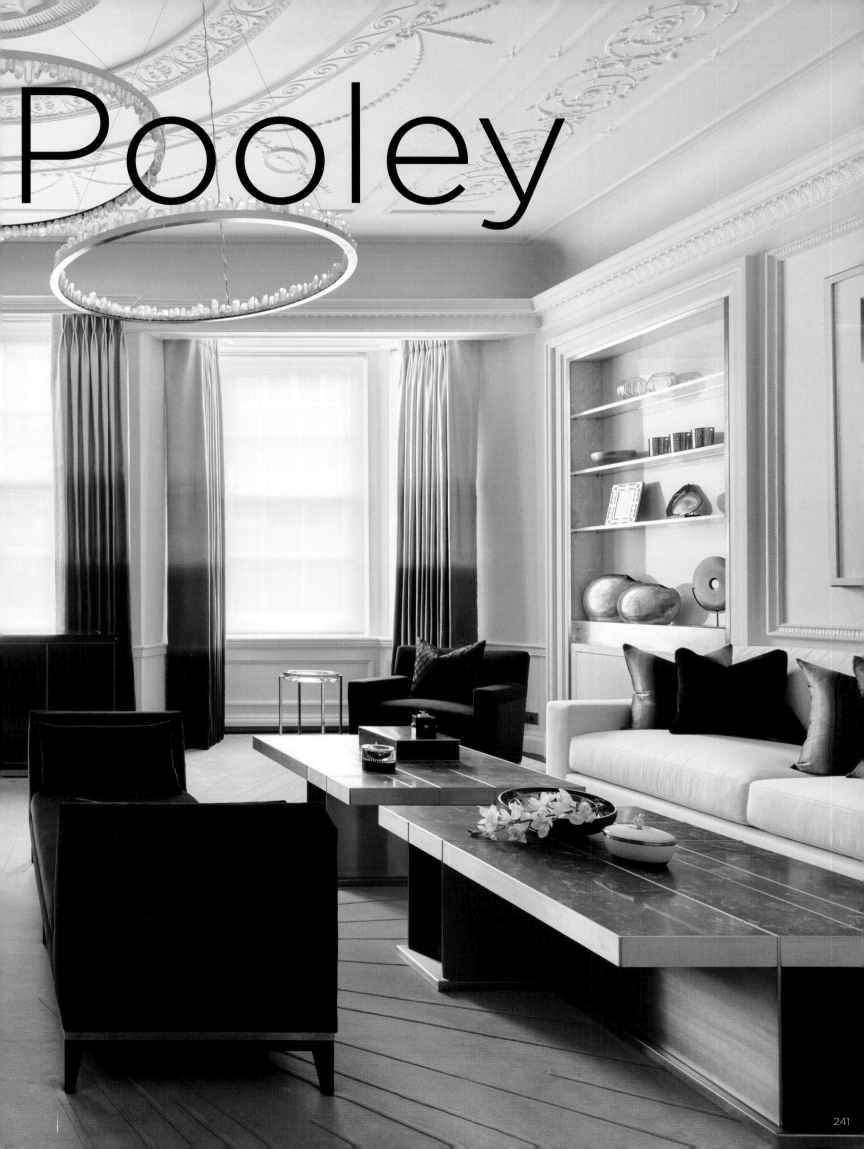

Designer: Katharine Pooley. Company: Katharine Pooley, London, UK. With a talented 40-strong team, Katharine Pooley produces some of the world's finest solutions for interiors, developments, architecture, yachts, private jets, furniture and product in the UK and overseas. Current work includes a cliff top villa in the South of France, private jet lounges in Colorado and Dubai and a contemporary 13,000 sq. ft. beach villa on the Palm in Dubai. Recently completed projects include a large villa in Kuwait, a private residence in Mayfair and a castle in Buckinghamshire. Design philosophy: realise the vision.

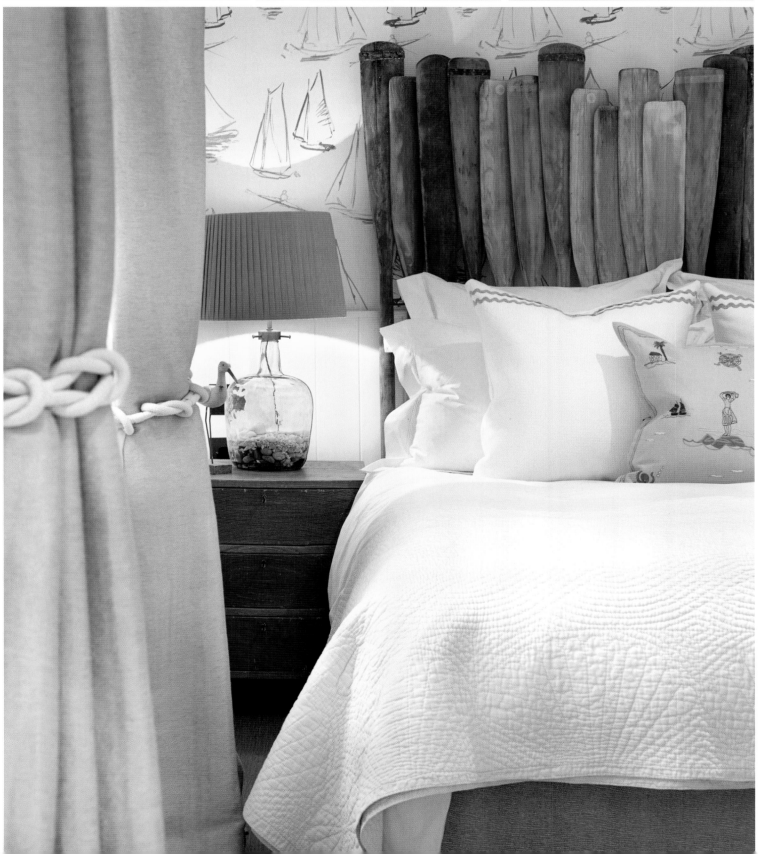

Ana Heleno
&
Simão Gibellino

Designers: Ana Heleno & Simão Gibellino. Company: Casazul - Creative Studio, Fátima, Portugal. Current projects include several private homes and apartments all over Portugal, a boutique beach hotel in the South of Portugal and a wedding destination villa in the centre of Portugal. Recent work includes a boutique hotel, a luxury residence for an Asian client and an organic restaurant & delicatessen. Design philosophy: happy projects for happy clients.

A SOUL EXPERIENCE

Bernd Gruber

Designer & Creative Director: Philipp Hoflehner. Company: Bernd Gruber, Kitzbühel, Austria. An international design brand, specialising in luxury, interior residential developments in Austria and overseas. Recent projects include a chalet in Jochberg, Oberhausenweg, a family house in Kitzbühel, Haslach and the company's own studio and showroom. Current work includes a townhouse in Berlin, a chalet in Kitzbühel and an apartment in Munich/Brunbach. Design philosophy: beauty, individuality, humanity.

SAARANHA&
VASCONCELOS

Designers: Rosario Tello & Carmo Aranha. Company: Saaranha&Vasconcelos, Lisbon, Portugal. A predominantly residential portfolio, with some commercial work, including private yachts. Recent projects include two luxury villas in Chengdu, China, a villa outside Lisbon, the architecture and interior design for a trendy boutique in Central Lisbon and a modern villa for a young family, also in Lisbon centre. Current projects include a luxury villa for an international client in Valle do Lobo, Algarve, a villa in Cascais, Portugal, a lakefront apartment in Zurich and a three storey villa in historic Lisbon. Design philosophy: dream to be different.

Designer: Krista Hartmann. Company: Krista Hartmann Interior AS, Oslo, Norway. Predominantly large residential projects as well as some commercial. Recent work includes a contemporary summer house by the Norwegian South coast, a family house in Oslo and a lodge in the mountains. Current projects include the conversion of an historic timber framed building near Oslo into a modern family home, both a contemporary and an old classical summer house by the sea and the company's own new office and showroom. Design philosophy: deliver projects with pride.

Krista Hartmann

A.N.D.

Designer: Ryu Kosaka (Executive Creative Director), Takashi Miyazato, Reiko Saito. Company: A.N.D. Aoyama Nomura Design, Tokyo, Japan. Specialising in retail, hospitality and residential design. Current work includes the retail design concept for an Italian luxury brand, a private residence in central Tokyo and a multi-tenant dining complex in Los Angeles. Recent projects include a twelve story medical complex in Tokyo, a four star hotel renovation in Seoul and Sushi-ichi Ginza in Jakarta. Design philosophy: everlasting design with a focus on detail.

Joanna Wood

Designer: Joanna Wood. Company: Joanna Wood Interior Design, London, UK. Recognised as one of Britain's leading figures in the international world of interior design. Current projects include a development for The Crown Estate in St James' London, the building of a new mews house in Belgravia and the restoration of a Gloucestershire manor house. Recent work includes The All England Lawn Tennis Club, a Covent Garden show flat and an apartment in New York. Design philosophy: quality, style, comfort.

Ray Wong

Designer: Ray Wong. Company: Guangzhou Ray Evolution Design, Guangzhou, China. Established in 2003, work is predominantly commercial, with recent examples including Dekang Club, Bump Restaurant & Bar and Song's Club.

Viterbo

Designer: Graçinha Viterbo. Viterbo Interior Design, Estoril, Portugal. Projects are international and award winning, predominantly in residential and hospitality design, as well as luxury developments. With their headquarters in Portugal and other offices in Angola and Singapore, they are soon to open in Qatar and London. Current projects include a 60 sq. mt. studio in St Germain, Paris, a 10,000 sq. m. home in Bangkok and a boutique hotel in the South of Portugal. Design philosophy: build backgrounds for memories.

LAUGH
Say Please & Thank
SHARE
IMAGINE MAKE BELIEVE
NO FUSSING BE KIND
WHINNING
FIGHTING
ACT SILLY
Dream Take Turns
Smile HAVE
GIGGLE FUN
Sing &
Dance PLAY

Joy Interiors

Designer: Chou-Yi. Company: Joy Interior Design Studio, Taiwan. Founded in 1989, with a concept, architecture studio created in 1995. Specialising in commercial projects including restaurants, teahouses, cafés, hotels, club houses and reception centres as well as public areas and private residences. Current projects include a BBQ restaurant called Umai Yakiniku, a Japanese style restaurant called Yimg Mo, plus Shih-Chi Stone Hotpot restaurant and Sushiraku seafood market restaurant. Design philosophy: the poetry of space.

MeC architetti

Designer: Serena Mignatti. Company: MeC architetti, Rome, Italy. A multi-disciplinary practice founded in 2014 by Serena Mignatti and Riccardo Crespi. Current projects include the renovation of a private penthouse in Lungotevere, near Tiberina Island, Rome, a penthouse on 5th Avenue, New York and a restaurant in Las Torres de Cotillas, Murcia, Spain. Recent work includes the renovation of a 20th Century, 300 sq. m. building in Rome, converted into a recording studio and a private music centre for well known pianists Katia and Marielle Labeque, an office renovation for the Impronta advertising agency in Rome and a penthouse in Murcia. Design philosophy: give a sense of belonging.

Louise Walsh

Designer: Louise Walsh. Company: Louise Walsh Interior Design & Decoration, NSW, Australia. Specialising in residential developments, marine design and resorts. Recent projects include a luxury beach house in Merewether Newcastle, a large family home in San Francisco and a historic home in Brisbane. Current work includes a luxury villa on Hamilton Island, a penthouse at Broadbeach Gold Coast and luxury homes in Brisbane and Sydney. Design philosophy: timeless, innovative, practical, customised.

Jack Lin

Designer: Jack Lin. Company: Wenge Hotel Space Design Consultants, Shenzhen, China. For 20 years Jack Lin has been a leading figure of pioneering design in the Asia-Pacific region, integrating both traditional and modern culture, in hotels, restaurants and club space. Current projects include a 21 room resort hotel in Dali, China, a 283 room boutique & luxury resort hotel beside lake Erhai in Dali, China and a boutique hotel in Zhejiang. Recent work includes Kairui·Guobao Hotel in Luoyang and Xi'an Garden Hotel beside the Great Wall in Beijing. Design philosophy: culture, harmony, balance.

Evolve

Designer: Raja Kabil. Company: Evolve Interiors, Cairo, Egypt. Predominantly luxury residential villas, hotels and commercial spaces. Current projects include a boutique hotel in Sharm Al Sheikh and villas in new Cairo. Recent work includes three villas in 6 October City, four villas in new Cairo and a hotel in Marrakech. Design philosophy: 'the difference is in the details'.

Designer: Aristos Migliaressis-Phocas. Company: A.M.P. INTERIORS (London, UK). Luxury design consultancy for an international clientele. Recent commissions include an artist's home in downtown Athens, a private residence at the Mandarin Oriental in London and the complete renovation of a townhouse in Fulham. Current projects include a new build, private villa in the hills of Athens, a family home in Monte Carlo and a bachelor pad in Chelsea. Design philosophy: 'nouveau chic' - reinvent the classics.

A.M.P. Interiors

Pang Xi

Designer: Pang Xi. Company: Suzhou XiShe Design & Consulting Ltd, Suzhou, China. Recent projects include the renovation of an old house in downtown Suzhou, a villa in the mountains in South China and a luxury apartment in Xintiandi, Shanghai. Design philosophy: beauty comes from life.

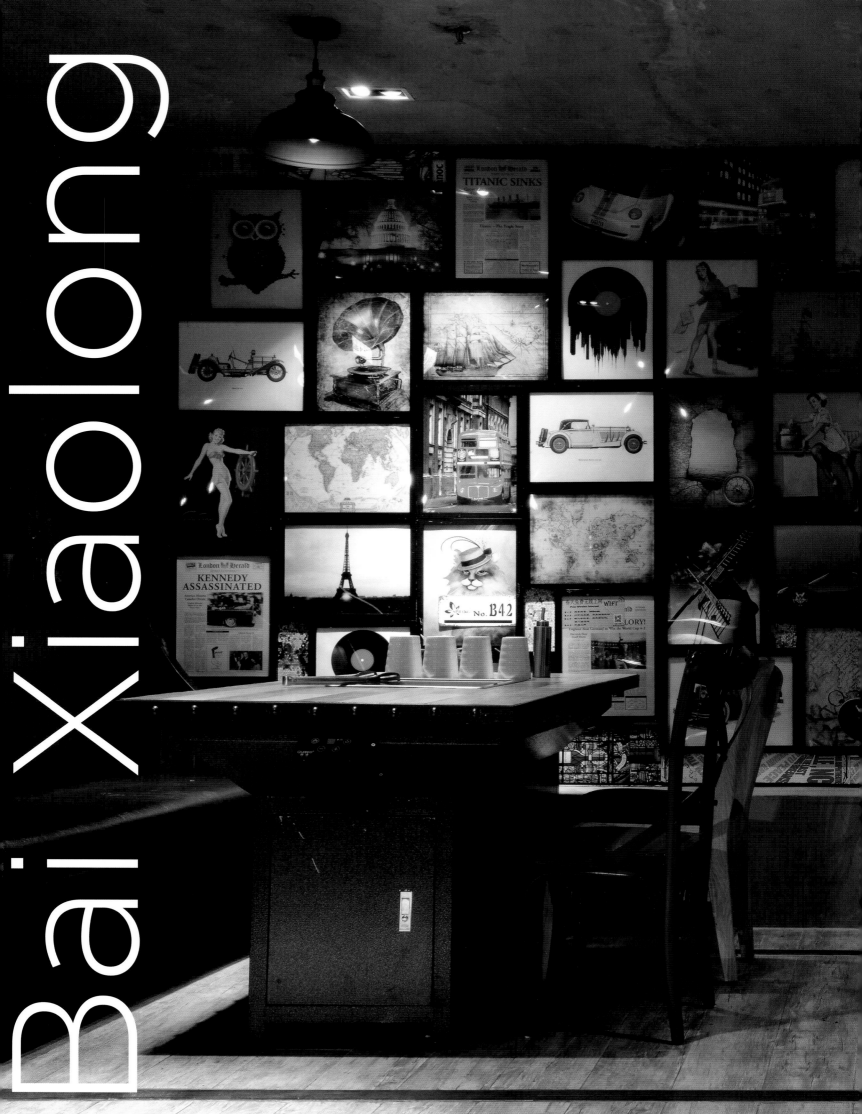

Bai Xiaolong

Designer: Bai Xiaolong. Company: Shanxi Yuan Create Design Studio, Shanxi Xiaodian, China. Current projects include Yingwujiang lifestyle store in Taiyuan, Haidao buffet restaurant in Taiyuan and Inout Fresh concept restaurant in Linfen. Design philosophy: art, life, design.

Jayne Wunder

Designer: Jayne Wunder. Company: Jayne Wunder Interior Design, London, UK. Specialising in luxury, primary and secondary, private homes and boutique hotels in the U.K. Cape Town and overseas. Current work includes a penthouse in Primrose Hill for overseas clients and a farmhouse style home in Cape Town in the wine region. Recent projects include a penthouse in Dubai. Design philosophy: fanatical about detail.

Idmen Liu

Designer: Idmen Liu. Company: Shenzhen Juzhen Mingcui Design, Shenzhen, China. Founded in 2010, the company provides high end design services with an international vision, throughout China. Recent projects include the office of Shenzhen Matrix Design and the office of Chongqing Vanke, plus the sales centre of Guangzhou Tianhe of China Resources Land Limited. Current work includes Jiang House of One Sino Park project of Shanghai Sunac, the sales centre of the Foshan Lecong Tengchong project and the exhibition centre for DOS office furniture. Design philosophy: keep walking on the road of design.

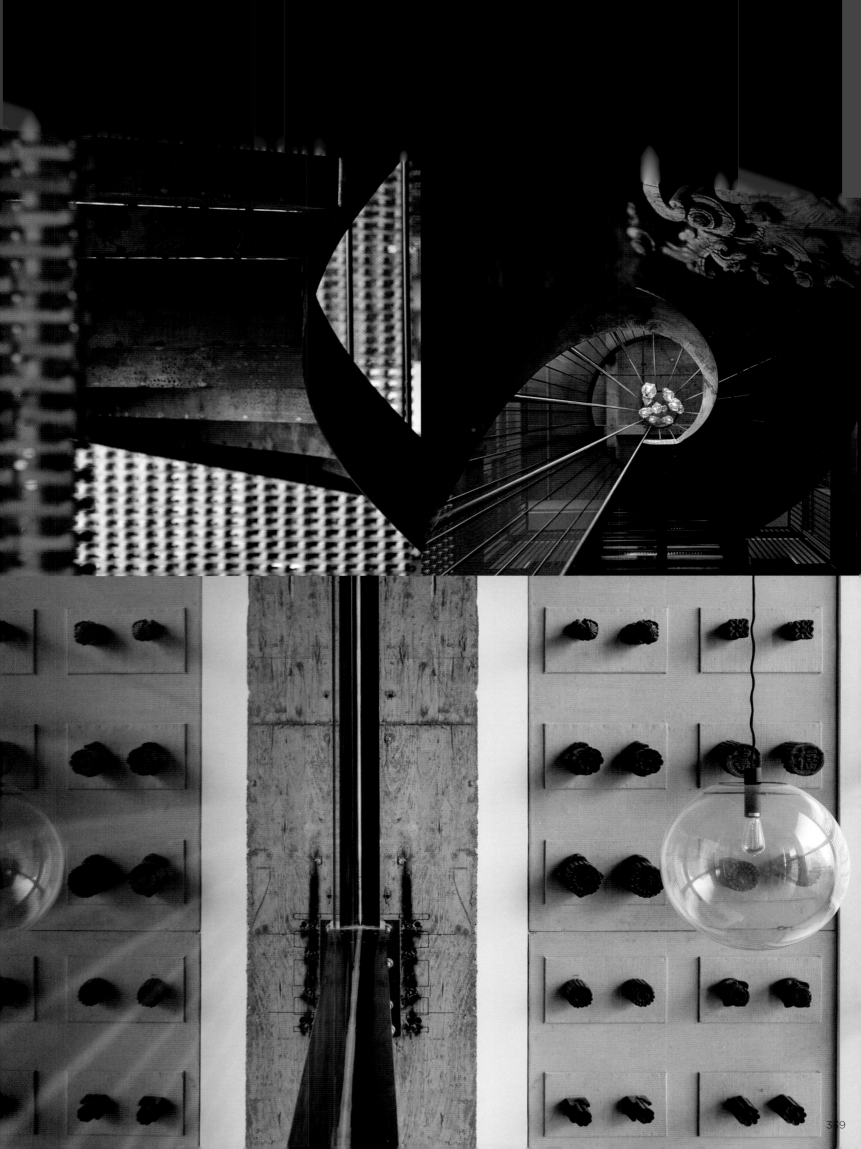

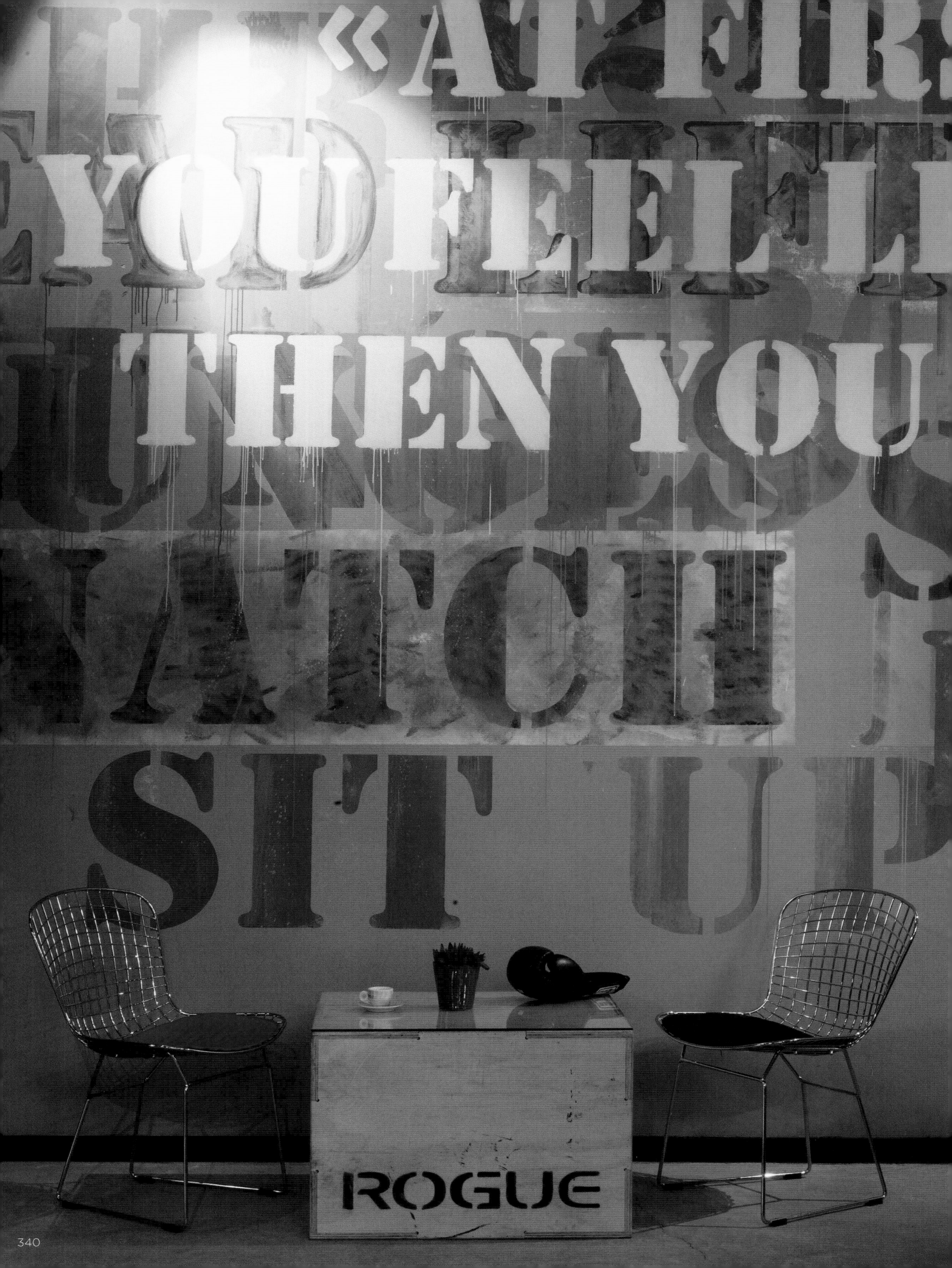
“AT FIR
YOU FEEL
THEN YOU
ATCH
SIT
ROGUE

Natalia Maslova

Designer: Natalia Maslova. Company: 3LDecor (Live, Love, Laugh), Moscow, Russia. Specialising in both public projects: restaurants, offices, sports facilities, showrooms and luxury interior design in Russia and overseas. Current projects include a villa and an apartment in Moscow and a retail store chain and villa in Voronezh. Recent work includes a 1,000 sq. m. cross-fit sports facility in Moscow, the design of a gastronomic restaurant in Moscow city and an executive office and apartment in Moscow. Design philosophy: live, love, enjoy.

Designer: Gulia Galeeva. Company: Gulia Galeeva Design, Moscow, Russia. Luxury homes, private jets and yachts all over the world, including New York, Miami, South of France and Moscow. Current projects include a spacious penthouse in downtown Moscow, overlooking the Kremlin and a family residence in the Moscow countryside. Recent work includes apartments in the centre of Moscow and a yacht design collaboration. Design philosophy: soulful, timeless, individual.

Gulia Galeeva

Taylor Howes

Designer: Karen Howes. Company: Taylor Howes, Knightsbridge, London, UK. An award winning international design practice consisting of a team of thirty designers, headed by Karen Howes, alongside her Creative Director Sandra Drechsler and Design Director Jane Landino. Current projects include a villa in Abu Dhabi, two large family houses in St. John's Wood and four show apartments in an exclusive Kensington development. Recent work includes an 18,000 sq. ft. house in Kensington, three show apartments in Regent's Park and show apartments in the heart of Mayfair. Design philosophy: caring, creative, above and beyond.

Michael Del Piero

Designer: Michael Del Piero. Company: Michael Del Piero Good Design, Chicago, USA. With an interior design studio and shop showcasing antique and unique finds. Current projects include a modern barn in Amagansett NY, a 7,200 sq. ft. home in Chicago's Lincoln Park neighbourhood and the complete renovation of a 1928 limestone home, situated on a small, wooded lake in Fond du Lac, Wisconsin. Recent projects include a 1920's Mediterranean style home in a Chicago suburb and a five story town house on the Chicago River. Design philosophy: serene with simple, ancient with modern, rough with luxurious.

Honky

Designer: Christopher Dezille. Company: Honky Interior Design and Architecture, London, UK. A multi award winning practice, offering a luxury comprehensive design service to private clients, property developers and boutique hotels in the UK and overseas. Current work includes a number of projects for developers, a substantial family home in Aberdeen, a penthouse in Putney with panoramic views of London and a family home in Fleet. Recent projects include a pied-à-terre in Westminster, a duplex penthouse in Aldwych and several apartments across London. Design philosophy: innovation, quality, service.

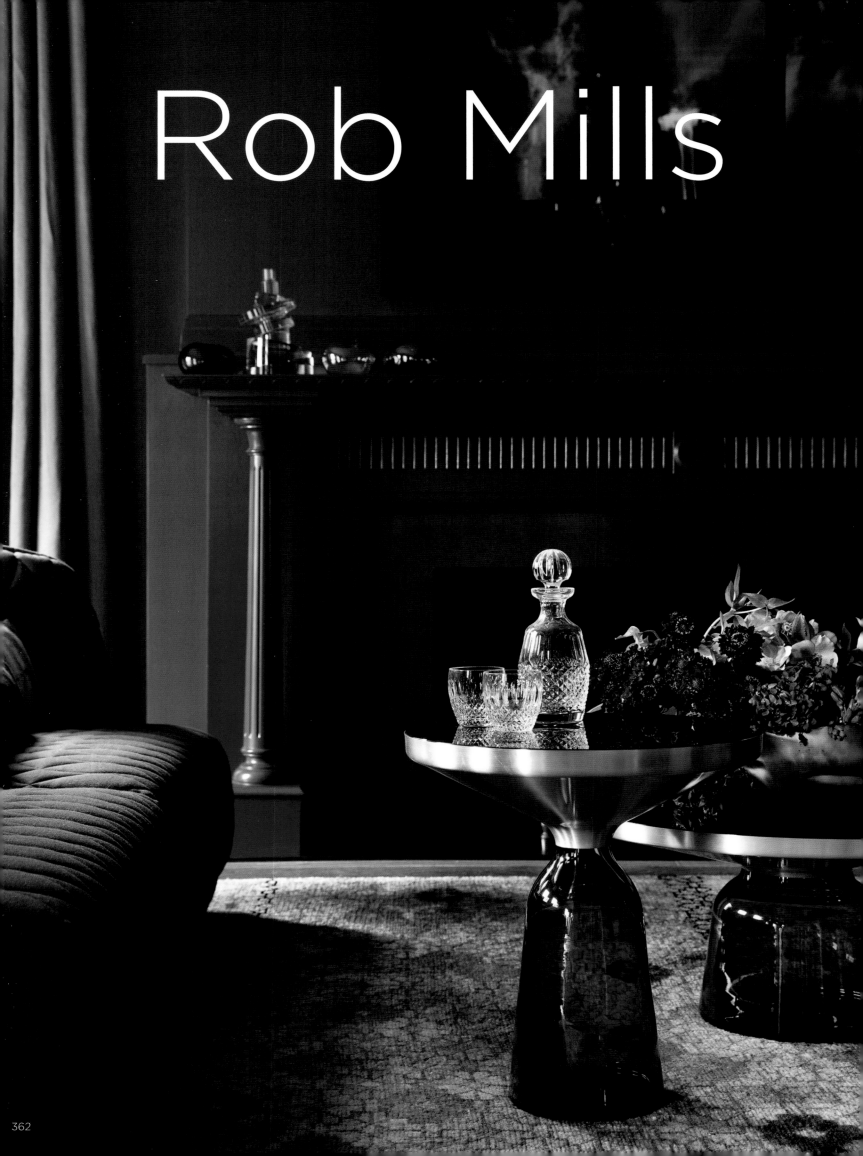

Rob Mills

Designer: Rob Mills. Company: Rob Mills Architects, Melbourne & Sydney, Australia. Specialising in creating residences that nurture the soul and inspire the mind. Recent projects include One Hot Yoga studio in Sydney, the restoration of Carrical house in Toorak, Melbourne and a South Yarra house, a contemporary new build in Melbourne. Recent projects include Rob's own family home in Armadale and a range of developments including tailored apartments and high end residential properties in Toorak. Design philosophy: bespoke.

Designer: Steve Leung. Company: Steve Leung Designers, Hong Kong. A team of 400 professionals, specialising in residential, commercial and hospitality design. Recent projects include One Park Shanghai, Harbour Pinnacle in Hong Kong and One Shenzhen Bay. Current work includes Masraf Al Rayan Head Office at Doha, Ping An International Finance Centre in Shenzhen and yoo Residence, Hong Kong. Design philosophy: design without limits.

Steve Leung

Designer: Lucia Valzelli. Company: Dimore di Lucia Valzelli, Brescia, Italy. Specialising in high end, tailored and predominantly residential projects, boutique hotels, spa and luxury restaurants in Europe. Current projects include the full refurbishment of a super yacht in the South of France, an exclusive restaurant in Venice and the complete restoration of an historic mansion. Recent work includes a series of modern and luxury lofts in the town centre, an eclectic family penthouse in the country and a large villa on Lake Iseo, North Italy. Design philosophy: a sense of quiet luxury.

Dimore Studio

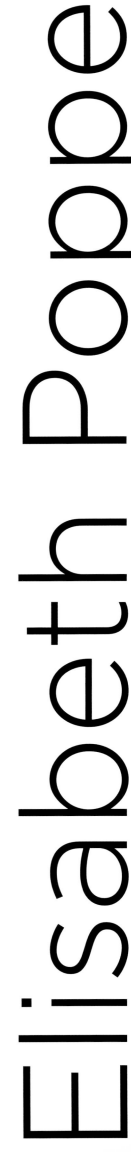

Designer: Elisabeth Poppe. Company: Poppe Design, Oslo, Norway. A small practice, specialising in high end private and commercial environments as well as luxury residential developments. Current projects include 3 townhouses and a waterfront apartment in Tjuvholmen, Oslo. Recent work includes a residential apartment building, a townhouse and the renovation of a 2 storey penthouse in Frogner, Oslo. Design philosophy: every project needs personality.

Oleg Klodt

Designers: Oleg Klodt and Anna Agapova. Company: Oleg Klodt Architecture & Design, Moscow, Russia. A luxury portfolio of private apartments and homes, hotels, restaurants and stores. Current projects include high end offices in a 7 storey tower, a penthouse in the heart of Moscow and private residences in Tashkent, Uzbekistan. Design philosophy: elegance is simplicity.

Sanjyt Syngh

Designer: Sanjyt Singh. Company: Sanjyt Syngh, New Delhi, India. Specialising in high end spaces in India, including residential interiors, private and weekend homes, boutique stores, restaurants and gyms. Current projects include a large, luxury office space in Mumbai, a beach mansion in Mangalore and a gym in Gurgaon (National Capital Region). Recent work includes a Swiss chateau inspired weekend home in Delhi and a luxury penthouse in Mumbai. Design philosophy: propelled by a love of design.

Rachel Laxer

Designer: Rachel Laxer. Company: Rachel Laxer Interiors, London, UK. Specialising in designing practical, luxurious and unexpected interiors for a variety of clients including professional athletes, sports team owners, financiers, entrepreneurs, internet executives, lawyers and artists in the UK and abroad. Current projects include a seaside house in Long Island, a residential home in Connecticut and a villa in California. Recent work includes a duplex in New York, an English country house and a penthouse in the heart of London. Design philosophy: practical, meticulous, luxurious, unexpected.

Allison Paladino

Designers: Allison Paladino ASID & Zita Rudd. Company: Allison Paladino Interior Design and Collections, Florida, USA. Specialising in bespoke interiors in South Florida and the Northeast. Allison also has a furniture line with EJ Victor, a hand cut glass lighting collection with Fine Art Lamps and a custom rug line with New River Artisans. Current projects include several homes on Palm Beach Island, including a three acre ocean front estate, merging several apartments together in New York City and a residence in Long Island. Recent work includes multiple homes in Palm Beach and several large ocean front condominiums. Design philosophy: listen well and bring the clients vision to reality.

THE FUTURE JUST HAPPENED.

Angelos

Designer: Angelos Angelopoulos. Company: Angelos Angelopoulos, Athens, Greece. Interior and exterior architecture, facade design and landscaping for private residences, urban & resort hotels, restaurants in Greece and overseas. Recent projects include a boutique hotel in Athens, the architectural and interior design of a residence in Athens and a hotel resort & spa in Corfu. Current work includes a luxurious resort in Mykonos, a hotel resort & spa in Cyprus and a hotel resort & spa in mainland Greece. Design philosophy: heal through the aesthetic.

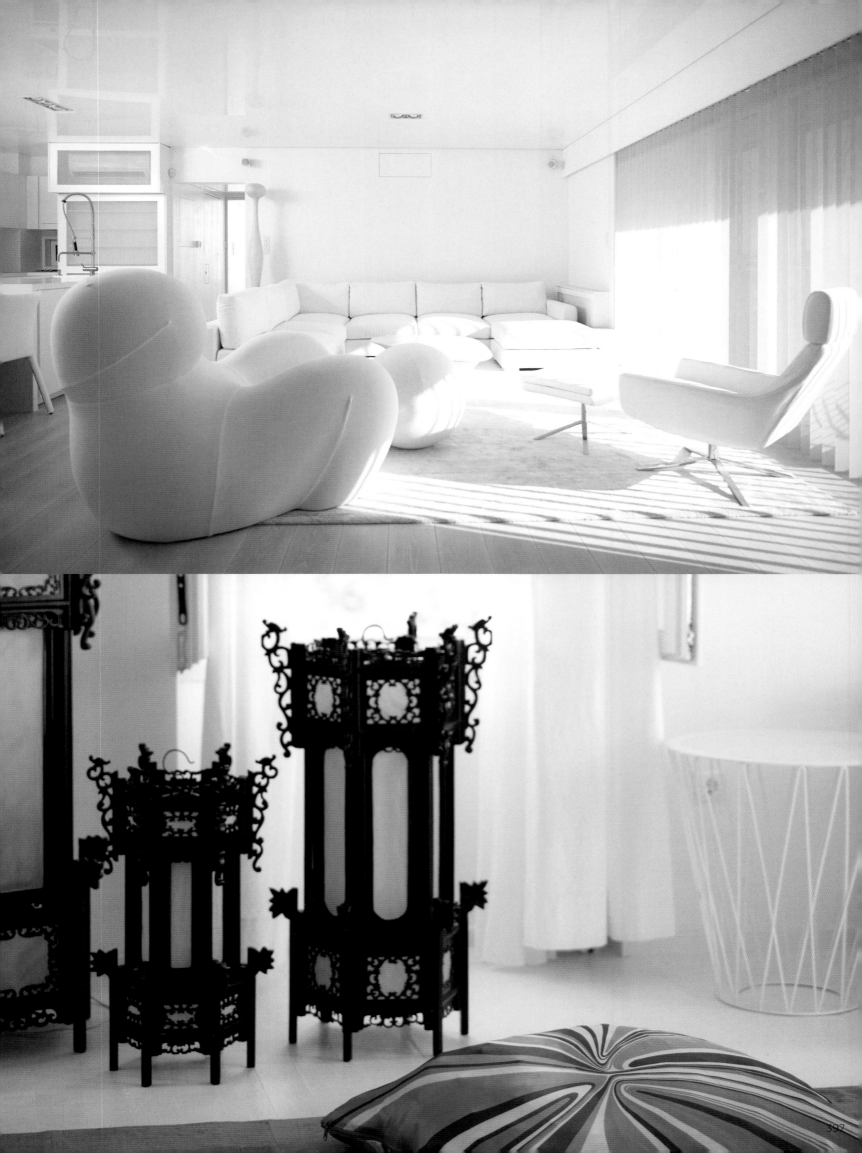

Branca

Designer: Alessandra Branca. Company: Branca, Chicago & New York. For the past 25 years, Branca has been a leading firm in luxury, bespoke residential work as well as for high profile hospitality and commercial projects. Current work includes a co-op in New York city, a chic rustic cabin in Colorado and a tropical beach house in Florida. Design philosophy: a joyful mix of a new classicism, chic practicality, elegance and wit.

Sophie Ashby

Designer: Sophie Ashby. Company: Studio Ashby Ltd, London, UK. Specialising in residential interior design in the UK and overseas, including both primary and secondary private homes as well as luxury residential developments, hotels and restaurants. Current projects include a boutique hotel in South Africa, a collection of limited edition penthouses in East London and a Nigerian restaurant in Marylebone. Recent work includes a mews house in St James's, a penthouse in Soho and a country house in Somerset. Design philosophy: authentic, eclectic, unique.

Arthur

McLaughlin

Designer: Arthur McLaughlin. Company: Arthur McLaughlin + Associates, California, USA. High end interiors for primary and secondary homes in the Bay Area and greater California. Recent projects include a mansion in San Francisco's Russian Hill neighbourhood, a contemporary renovation in Silicon Valley, a family residence in Pacific Heights and a new high rise in the Soma area of San Francisco. Current work includes a multiple structure weekend estate in the wine country, the design and renovation of a vacation home in Sebastopol and the updating of two urban apartments for a philanthropist and collector. Design philosophy: comfort defines luxury.

Designer: Prasetio Budhi. Company: Plus Design, Jakarta, Indonesia. Current projects include a private residential complex, a show apartment in Surabaya and contributing to a national exhibition, 'The Colours of Indonesia'. Recent work includes a luxury mansion in South Jakarta, a set of exclusive condominiums and several large family homes. Design philosophy: personality, simplicity, elegance.

Claudia Pelizzari

Designer: Claudia Pelizzari. Company: Claudia Pelizzari Interior Design, Brescia, Italy. Since opening her studio in 1991, Claudia's portfolio spans over 200 projects; including private residences, hotels and restaurants, for a cosmopolitan clientele. Current projects include a luxury apartment in Trocadero, Paris, a Japanese restaurant in Milan, a rhiad in Marrakesh and various city apartments in Italy. Design philosophy: tailored, timeless, professional.

Geraldine Milsom

Designer: Geraldine Milsom. Milsom Hotels, Essex, UK. Specialising in hotel and restaurant interior and exterior for boutique hotels. Current projects include The Pier restaurant on the Essex coast in Harwich, the complete redesign of the ground floor of Milsoms Hotel in Dedham and the refurbishment of the bedrooms and sitting room at the luxury hotel, Maison Talbooth. Design philosophy: blend contemporary with traditional, retain the original.

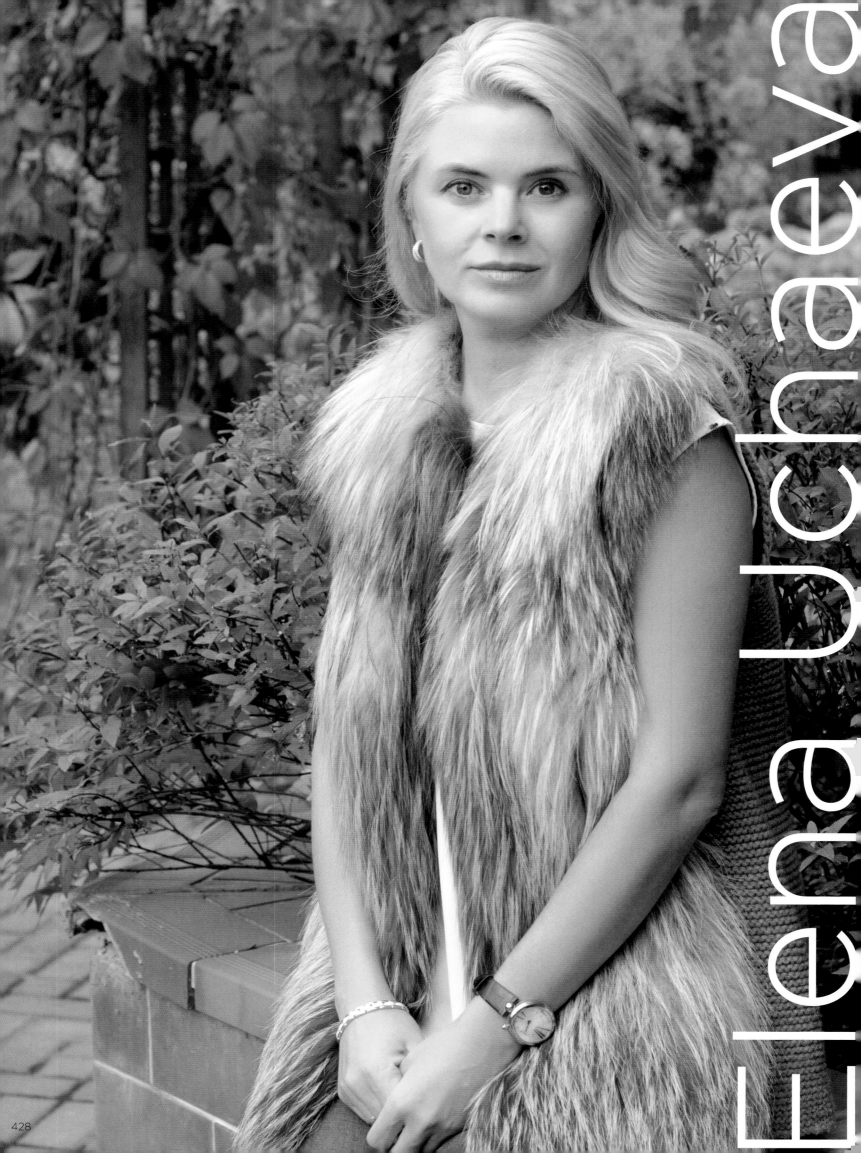

Elena Uchaeva

Designer: Elena Uchaeva. Company: Blue Jay Interior Design, Moscow, Russia. Specialising in residential and offices in St Petersburg, Moscow and Cyprus. Recent work includes a private apartment in St Petersburg, a house near Moscow, a villa in Cyprus and an office in Moscow city. Design philosophy: be intuitive, be inspired.

Kunihide Oshinomi

Designer: Kunihide Oshinomi. Company: k/o design studio, Tokyo, Japan. Covering residential interiors to skyscraper design, in collaboration with professionals around the world. Current work includes a rural complex of seaside cafés, a bar and hotel and luxury penthouse interiors in condominium towers located in Central Tokyo. Design philosophy: amaze.

COLLETT-
ZARZYCKI

Designers: Anthony Collett and Andrzej Zarzycki. Company: Collett Zarzycki Ltd, London, UK. A 25 year old architectural design practice which employs a team of 20, plus a large network of outside specialists, artists and crafts people. Current projects include the interior architecture and interior design in The Glebe, Chelsea; several private residences and show flats within Holland Green, Kensington and a private chalet in Switzerland. Recent work includes the interior architecture of a listed country manor house; the architecture and interior design for a family home in Corsica; the architecture, interior design and landscaping of a large private home in the South of France and the interior architecture and finishing of a lateral conversion spanning four buildings in Eaton Square. Design philosophy: respect the context, reflect the contemporary, incorporate the innovative.

Design Post

Designer: Jumpei Yamagiwa. Company: Design Post, Tokyo, Japan. Specialising in restaurants, bars and high end residential projects in Japan and overseas. Current projects include a boutique hotel and a steak restaurant in Japan and high end residential projects in Hong Kong. Recent work includes a Japanese restaurant, a beer restaurant and a Brazilian churrasco restaurant in Japan. Design philosophy: flexible, balanced, imbued with the spirit of Japanese art.

Olga Zubova

Designer: Olga Zubova. Company: ZDesign Studio, Moscow, Russia. Specialising in luxury private homes, hunting lodges, historic buildings, residential developments and small luxury hotels in Russia, France, Monaco and Italy. Current projects include an outstanding penthouse in Monaco, hunting residences in Central Russia and the restoration of a 19th Century residence in the heart of Moscow. Recent work includes a private residence in Monaco, the renovation of a chateaux in the Loire, France and country houses in Moscow. Design philosophy: individual without compromise.

Alexander James

Designer: Stacey Sibley, Creative Director. Alexander James Interior Design, London, UK. Delivering a complete service for luxury developers and high end residential clients in London and the Home Counties. Recent projects include a luxury family home in the heart of Knightsbridge, a 7,000 sq. ft. regency style townhouse in Hampstead and a deluxe penthouse apartment in Westminster. Current work includes a villa in the Algarve, a 23,000 sq. ft. mansion on the Wentworth Estate, an 18,000 sq. ft. family home on St George's Hill and a Hilton Hotel in Minsk, Belarus. Design philosophy: exceed expectation.

Beijing Newsdays

457

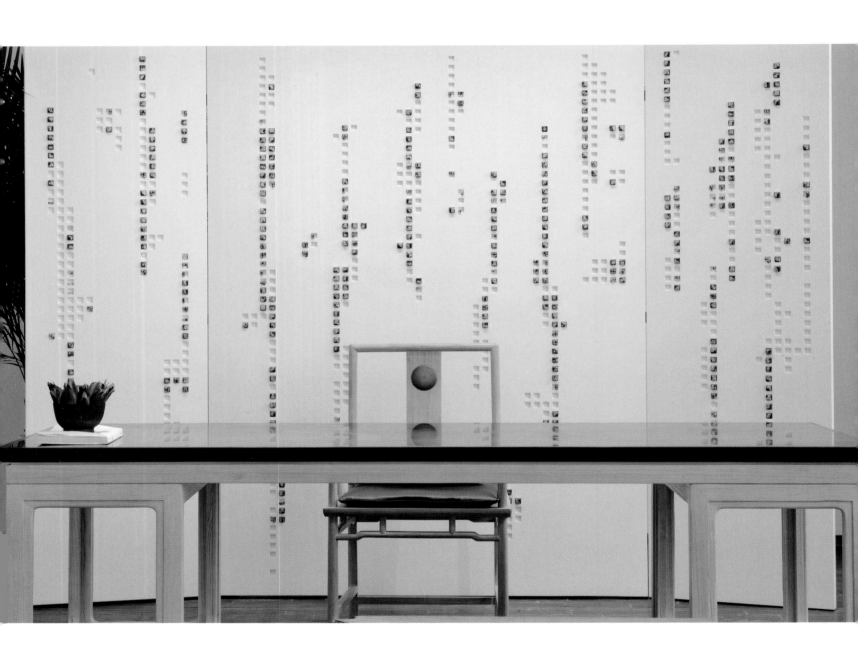

Designers: Jianguo Liang, Wenqi Cai, Yiqun Wu, Junye Song, Tingyu Liu, Chunkai Nei. Company: Beijing Newsdays, Beijing, China. Engaged in the design of various projects including high end hotels, clubhouses, restaurants, mock-ups, cultural and commercial spaces. Current work includes Wen Chong Hall of the Forbidden City, the third of the Forbidden City College series, Xi Huang Sheng Di Meijing Suxin garden, LvCheng JiangNanLi inter clubhouse and Henan Kaifeng HuiXian clubhouse. Design philosophy: solutions beyond expectations.

Eric Kuster

Designer: Eric Kuster. Company: Eric Kuster Metropolitan Luxury, Huizen, The Netherlands. Specialising in residential, commercial, yacht and hotel projects including exclusive, interior design products under the Metropolitan Luxury label. Recent projects include a custom built yacht in Antibes, South of France, designed in partnership with Ferretti yacht builders, a cliff top house in Altea, Spain with 180 degree sea views and a luxury, Geneva lakeside villa with spa, gym, pool and cinema housed in the basement. Current work includes a city apartment and private members club in Amsterdam and private villas in Dubai. Design philosophy: exceed expectation: it has to be perfect.

Sophie Paterson

Designer: Sophie Paterson. Sophie Paterson Interiors, Surrey, UK. Luxury, residential interiors in the UK and overseas for both private clients and developers. Current work includes a Grade II listed apartment in Knightsbridge, a 13,000 sq. ft. new build house in Chelmsford and several private residences in Surrey. Recent projects include a penthouse in Chelsea, two 10,000 sq. ft. show homes in Surrey and a 12,000 sq. ft. house in Wentworth. Design philosophy: timeless, luxurious, practical.

Bo Li

Designer: Bo Li. Company: Cimax Design Engineering, Shenzhen, China. Working predominantly on private mansions, hotels, clubs and offices. Current projects include an 850 sq. m. villa in Shenzhen, a private club and a design hotel in Xili lake resort, Shenzhen. Design philosophy: customer centred.

Hill House

Designers: Jenny Weiss & Helen Bygraves. Company: Hill House Interiors, Weybridge, Surrey, UK. An award winning, international practice, supported by a 20 strong team of designers and architects, along with an office in Monte-Carlo and lifestyle showrooms in Chelsea and Weybridge. Recent projects include a 30,000 sq. ft. private, ambassadorial residence with 6,000 sq. ft. spa, on The Wentworth Estate, a 12,000 sq. ft. family home, a refurbished town house in Chelsea and an investment duplex apartment in Belgravia. Current work includes two projects in the Bahamas; one overlooking the marina, the other a luxury golf course residence, a lateral town house conversion on Kings Road, Chelsea, an apartment in Dubai and several large, private, family residences in Surrey. Design philosophy: 'you only get one chance to make a first impression.'

Elena Akimova

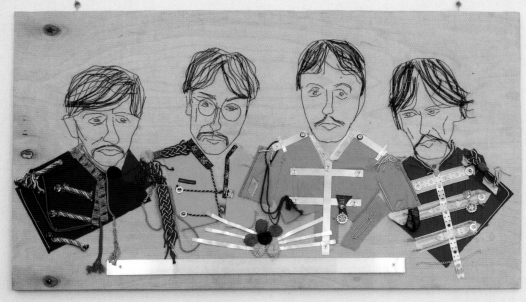

Designer: Elena Akimova & Ekaterina Andreeva.
Company: Elena Akimova Design, Austria & Russia.
Specialising in the luxury interiors of private homes,
galleries, exhibitions, conceptual interiors and a
private jet, in France, Austria, Spain and Russia.
Current projects include a villa in the South of
France, a private psychiatric practice in Vienna and
an apartment in Moscow. Recent work includes a
villa in Ibiza, a penthouse in Vienna and two large
apartments in Moscow. Design philosophy: live and
work with humour and imagination.

Anna Bilton

Designer: Anna Bilton. Company: Anna Bilton Limited, London, UK. Offering a highly creative and fully comprehensive, luxury interior design service. Recent projects include a substantial new build waterfront home and guest house in the Bahamas, the extensive refurbishment of a Grade II listed Georgian house in Oxfordshire and a large apartment in Zurich. Current work includes the re-modelling of a large townhouse in Kensington, an orangery extension and wing conversion of a Grade II listed house in Buckinghamshire, a ski chalet in Verbier and traditional equestrian facilities and apartments in Berkshire. Design philosophy: reflect personality, compliment lifestyle, make dreams a reality.

Arent&Pyke

Designers: Juliette Arent & Sarah-Jane Pyke. Company: Arent&Pyke, Sydney, Australia. Current projects include various residential projects across Sydney, including the substantial renovation of a house on the Northern Beaches, updating an inner city worker's cottage and collaboration with architects to furnish and decorate a new luxury harbour side home. Recent work includes a boutique hotel in Perth, an interpretation of a classic beach house at Macmasters Beach on the NSW Central Coast and a tailored solution for a family home in Double Bay in Sydney's Eastern Suburbs. Design philosophy: enrich people's lives.

Hirsch Bedner

Designer: David T'Kint. Company: Hirsch Bedner Associates (HBA), Dubai, UAE. Established in 1965, HBA is the world's leading global hospitality interior design firm, with more than 1,800 designers across 25 offices nationwide. Specialising in hotels, resorts, casinos and spas. Recent projects include Raffles in Jakarta, Four Seasons, Abu Dhabi and Tangla, Brussels, a 187 room, five star property for Tangla Hotels and Resorts. Current work includes Langham,

Jeddah, Langham Place, Dubai, Fairmont, Lagos, The Biltmore, Riyadh, Saudi Arabia, Curio by Hilton, Dubai and Jumeirah, Aqaba, Jordan. Design philosophy: to rewrite the language of design with each new project, remaining agile and responsive to the landscape.

Designers: Nikki Hunt and Andrea Savage. Company: Design Intervention, Singapore. A multi award winning studio, specialising in luxury residential and boutique commercial projects throughout the Asia Pacific region. Current work includes a penthouse apartment in Bangkok, a boutique hotel in Japan, a private family complex in Singapore and a destination bar & lounge in Singapore. Recent projects include an elegant Singapore penthouse, a private apartment in Sydney and a luxurious villa in Phuket. Design philosophy: to craft bespoke interiors which resonate with personality.

Design Intervention

Fiona Barratt-Campbell

Designer: Fiona Barratt-Campbell. Company: Fiona Barratt Interiors, London, UK. Established in 2006, Fiona Barratt Interiors caters for the world's most affluent clientele, delivering exceptional interior design for luxury residential and commercial developments. Recent projects include a manor house in Kent, a development show apartment in London and a villa in Mallorca. Current work includes a substantial family home in Bath, 92 commercial apartments in Moscow and hotel penthouses in Hong Kong. Design philosophy: by understanding the aspirations of the client and working with existing elements of space, the outcome is an interior which tells a story and reflects the client's individuality.

4 Nicky Haslam
Nicky Haslam Studio
#1, 165 Cromwell Road
London, UK, SW5 OSQ
Tel: +44 (0)207 730 3100
info@nickyhaslamstudio.com
www.nickyhaslamstudio.com

14 Vincent Van Duysen
Vincent Van Duysen Architects
Lombardenvest 34
2000 Antwerp, Belgium
Tel: +32 3 205 9190
Fax +32 3 204 0138
info@vincentvanduysen.com
www.vincentvanduysen.com

20 Chris Browne & Debra Fox
Fox Browne Creative
PO Box 2826, Saxonwold,
Johannesburg
2132 South Africa
Tel: +27 11 440 9357
www.foxbrowne.com

28 Cindy Rinfret
Rinfret, Ltd. Interior Design &
Decoration
354 Greenwich Avenue
Greenwich
CT 06830 USA
Tel:+203 622 000
info@rinfretltd.com
www.rinfretltd.com

36 Chang, Ching-Ping
Tienfun Interior Planning Co. Ltd
12F, No. 211 Chung Min Rd
North Dist, Taichung City
Taiwan, R.O.C.
Tel: +886 4 220 18 908
Fax: + 886 4 220 36 910
tf@mail.tienfun.tw
www.tienfun.com.tw

42 Kim Stephen
Kim Stephen Interiors
Unit 14, 1 Rocks Lane
London SW13 0DB
Tel: +44 7407 320001
kim@kimstephen.com
www.kimstephen.com

48 Stephen Ryan
Stephen Ryan Design and Decoration
7 Clarendon Cross
Holland Park W11 4AP UK
Tel: +44 (0)20 7243 0864
info@stephenryandesign.com
www.stephenryandesign.com

56 Aleksandra Laska
Ul Krakowskie Przedmieście 85m 5
00-079 Warsaw
Poland
Tel: +48 22 826 0796
Tel: +48 609 522 942
aleksandra.laska@gmail.com

66 Erin Martin
Erin Martin Design
1118 Hunt Avenue
St. Helena, CA 94574, USA
Tel: +707 963 4141
Martin Showroom
1350 Main Street
St. Helena, CA 94574, USA
Tel: +707 967 8787
www.erinmartindesign.com

72 Dan Menchions & Keith Rushbrook
II BY IV DESIGN
77 Mowat Avenue
Suite 109
Toronto
Ontario
M6K 3E3 Canada
design@iibyiv.com
www.iibyiv.com

78 Kot Ge
LSD CASA
305 Block C3
OTC-Loft Nanshan District
ShenZhen
China
Tel: +86 755 86106060
zml@lsdcasa.com
www.lsdcasa.com

82 Jan Showers
Jan Showers & Associates
1308 Slocum Street
Dallas
Texas 75207, USA
Tel: +214 747 5252
Fax: +214 747 5242
natalie@janshowers.com
www.janshowers.com

90 Stefano Dorata
Studio Dorata
00197 Roma
12a/14 Via Antonio Bertoloni, Italy
Tel: +39 (0)68084747
Fax: +39 (0)68077695
studio@stefanodorata.com
www.stefanodorata.com

94 Cui Shu
New Look Design Co. Ltd.
No. 16 Mao Long Cultural and Creative
Industrial Park, No. 1,
Sanjianfang East Road, Chaoyang Dist,
Beijing, China
Tel: +86 18610094665
502337509@qq.com
www.69nkd.com

100 Jorge Canete
Interior Design Philosophy
Domaine de la Chartreuse de La
Lance, CH - 1426 Concise (VD),
Switzerland
Tel: +41 78 710 25 34
info@jorgecanete.com
www.jorgecanete.com

106 Gang Cao & Yanan Yan
Henan Erheyong Architectural
Decoration Design Co., Ltd
No129, the three road north second
street intersection
Jingkai area of Zhengzhou
Henan Province, China
Tel:+86 371 633 80939
Mobile:+86 138 37180399
13837180399@163.com
www.ehydesign.com

112 Anna Spiro
Black & Spiro Interior Design
768 Brunswick Street
New Farm Qld., 4005 Australia
Tel:+617 3254 3000
info@blackandspiro.com.au
www.blackandspiro.com.au

118 Toni Espuch
AZULTIERRA
C/Córcega 276-282
08008 Barcelona, Spain
Tel/Fax: +34 932 178 356
azultierra@azultierra.es
www.azultierra.es

124 Tomoko Ikegai
Ikg Inc.
210 Building 2-1-5-3F
Shimomeguro, Meguro-ku
Tokyo, Japan 150-0064
Tel: +81 3 6417 4817
Fax: +81 3 6417 4816
info@ikg.cc
www.ikg.cc

132 Kelly Hoppen
Kelly Hoppen Interiors
Unit 5, Vencourt Place
London, UK, W6 9NU
Tel: +44 20 7471 3350
info@kellyhoppen.co.uk
www.kellyhoppeninteriors.com

140 Gisbert Pöppler
Gisbert Pöppler Architektur Interieur
Falckensteinstrasse 48
10997 Berlin, Germany
Tel: +49 30 4404 4973
mail@gisbertpoeppler.com
www.gisbertpoeppler.com

144 Katsunori Suzuki &
Eiichi Maruyama
Fantastic Design Works Co., Ltd
2nd fl. 3-6-5 Jingumae, Shibuya-ku,
Tokyo 150-0001 Japan
Tel: +81 3 6455 5080
maruyama@f-fantastic.com
www.f-fantastic.com

150 Zeynep Fadillioglu
Zeynep Fadillioglu Design
Amiral Fahri Engin Sok. No: 3
34470 Rumelihisari
Istanbul, Turkey
Tel: +90 212 287 0936
design@zfdesign.com,
www.zfdesign.com

156 Ajax Law Ling Kit &
Virginia Lung Wai Ki
One Plus Partnership Limited
Unit 1604, 16th Floor
Eastern Centre, 1065 King's Road,
Hong Kong
Tel: +852 259 19 308
admin@onepluspartnership.com
www.onepluspartnership.com

160 Meryl Hare
Hare + Klein
91 Bourke Street
Woolloomooloo
Sydney 2011
Australia
Tel: +612 9368 1234
Fax: +612 9368 1020
info@hareklein.com.au
www.hareklein.com.au

166 Enis Karavil
Sanayi 313 Architects
Atatürk Oto Sanayi Sitesi 2. Kısım 10.
Sokak No:313 Maslak/Istanbul.
Tel: +90212 286 38 57
ask@sanayi313.com
www.sanayi313.com

172 Christina Sullivan Roughan
Roughan Interior Design
78 Godfrey Road West
Weston, CT 06883 USA
Tel: +(203) 769-1150
Fax: +(203) 769-1151
info@roughaninteriors.com
www.roughaninteriors.com

178 Yu Ping, Xidian University,
Building No 3
Huangjia Garden, Gaoxin Road
Yanta District, Xi'an City
Shanxi Province, China
Tel: +86 15829549626
Fax: +86(29)84501719
dacai-119@163.com

184 Glenn Gissler
Glenn Gissler Design
1123 Broadway #1100
New York
NY 10010 USA
Tel: +212-228-9880 info@GISSLER.com
www.GISSLER.com

190 Geir Oterkjaer
Slettvoll Sthlm
Regeringsgatan 12
11153 Stockholm
Sweden
Tel: +46 8 214 170
geir.oterkjaer@gmail.com
www.slettvoll.se

194 Li Zurong & Bjoern Rechtenbach
Season Interior Design
Lane 236, No. 1000
Jiuting Town
Songjiang District
Shanghai, China
Tel/Fax: +86(21)67635251
42504109@qq.com

200 Suzanne Lovell
Suzanne Lovell Inc.
225 West Ohio Street, Suite 200,
Chicago, Illinois, 60654
USA
Tel: +312 598 1980
contact@suzannelovellinc.com
www.suzannelovellinc.com

206 Rosarinho Gabriel
Coisas da Terra - Arte e decoração
Lda. Avenida Dr. Brandão de
Vasconcelos, 31 Almoçageme
2705-019 Colares
Portugal
Tel: +351 21 928 03 62
Fax: +351 21 928 02 84
decor@coisasdaterra.pt
www.coisasdaterra.pt

212 Tianqi Guan, Lei Jin
Evolution Design
#17 Yinghuayuan
Yinghua West Street
Chaoyang District
Beijing 100029
China
Tel: +86-10-84109696
www.evolutiondesign.com.cn

216 Kim Scodro
Kim Scodro Interiors
303 East Wacker Drive, Suite 1130,
Chicago, Illinois 60601
USA
Tel: +312 925 8023
info@kimscodro.com
www.kimscodro.com

220 Lígia Casanova
Atelier Lígia Casanova
Rua das Praças, 30-3
1200-767 Lisboa, Portugal
Tel: +351 919 704 583
atelier@ligiacasanova.com
www.ligiacasanova.com

224 Pippa Paton
Pippa Paton Design Ltd
West Wing
Old Berkshire Hunt Kennels
Oxford Road, Kingston Bagpuize,
Oxfordshire OX13 5AP
Tel: +44 (0) 1865 595470
Mobile: +44 (0) 7836 793624
studio@pippapatondesign.co.uk,
www.pippapatondesign.co.uk

230 Yasumichi Morita
GLAMOROUS co.,ltd.
Aoyama Tower Bldg.
10F 2-24-15 Minamiaoyama
Minato-ku, Tokyo 107-0062, Japan
Tel: +81 3 5414 3930
info@glamorous.co.jp
www.glamorous.co.jp

234 Greg Natale
Greg Natale Design
62 Buckingham Street
Surry Hills NSW
2010 Australia
Tel: +61 2 8399 2103
info@gregnatale.com
www.gregnatale.com

240 Katharine Pooley
Katharine Pooley Ltd
160 Walton Street
London SW3 2JL, UK
Tel: +44 207 584 3223
enquiries@katharinepooley.com
www.katharinepooley.com

252 Ana Heleno & Simão Gibellino
Casazul - Creative Studio
Rua Santa Luzia
19 – Apartado 327
Moita Redonda – 2495/650 Fatima
Portugal
Tel: +351 916 003 733/23
www.casazulstudio.pt

256 Philipp Hoflehner
Bernd Gruber GmbH
Pass-Thurn-Strasse 8
A-6371 Aurach-Kitzbuhel
Austria
Tel: +43 5356 711 01-0
atelier@bernd-gruber.at
www.bernd-gruber.at

260 Carmo Aranha & Rosario Tello
Saaranha & Vasconcelos
Rua Vale Formoso
45, 1950-279 Lisbon, Portugal
Tel: +351 21 845 3070
Tel: +351 21 849 5325
info@saaranhavasconcelos.pt
www.saaranhavasconcelos.pt

264 Krista Hartmann
Krista hartmann Interior AS
Kristinelundveien 6
0268 Oslo, Norway
Tel: +47 970 64 654
krista@krista.no www.krista.no

270 Ryu Kosaka
(Executive Creative Director)
Takashi Miyazato, Reiko Saito
A.N.D. Aoyama Nomura Design
Qiz Aoyama 3F, 3-39-5
Jingumae, Shibuya-ku, Tokyo
150-0001 Japan
Tel: +81 3 5412 6785
www.and-design.jp

274 Joanna Wood
Joanna Wood Interior Design
7 Bunhouse Place
London SW1W 8HU
Tel: +44 207 730 0693
Fax: +44 207 730 4135
info@joannawood.com
www.joannawood.com

280 Ray Wong
Guangzhou Ray Evolution Design
Co. Ltd. Room 201
NO.33, Street Six
Liuyun, Tianhe District
Guangzhou, China
Tel: +86 (20)37638510
raye@raye.hk
www.raye.hk

286 Gracinha Viterbo
Viterbo Interior Design
Avenida de Nice
68, 2765-259 Estoril, Portugal &
Europe-Asia-Africa-Middle East
Tel: +351 214 646 240
Fax: +351 214 646 249
info@viterbo-id.com
www.viterbo-id.com

292 Chou-Yi
Joy Interior Design Studio
No.204, Sec. 1
Wuquan W. Rd., West Dist.
Taichung City 403
Taiwan (R.O.C.)
Tel : +886 4 23759455
joyis.chou@msa.hinet.net
www.joychou.com

298 Serena Mignatti
MeC architetti
Via della Stazione Vaticana 5
00165 Rome, Italy
Tel: +39 06638 2355
info@mec-architetti.com
www.mec-architetti.com

302 Louise Walsh
Louise Walsh Interior Design
& Decoration
4/64 Ballina St, Lennox Head
NSW Australia 2478
Tel: +612 6687 5010
Mobile: +61 420 812 640
info@louisewalsh.com.au
www.louisewalsh.com.au

306 Jack Lin
Wenge Hotel Space Design
Consultants Ltd
Room 602, Block A, Future Plaza,
No.4060, Qiaoxiang Road
Nanshan District, Shenzhen,
Guangdong
China
Tel: +86 (0)755 2666 6880
Fax: +86(0)755 2666 6289
sz26666880@126.com
www.wg-space.com

310 Raja Kabil
Evolve Interiors
15 Moudiriet El Tahrir St
Garden City, Cairo, Egypt
Tel: +2 02 2794 7741
info@evolve-designs.com
www.evolve-designs.com

316 Aristos Migliaressis-Phocas
A.M.P. Interiors
130 Finborough Road
London SW10 9AQ, UK
Tel: +44 (0) 77 9276 2715
info@amp-interiors.com
www.amp-interiors.com

322 Pang Xi
Pang Xi Design Consultants Co. Ltd.
Block #C7, 859 Pan Xu Rd
Suzhou, China
Tel: +86 512 6812 1510
xishe@vip.126.com

326 Bai Xiaolong
Shanxi Yuan Create Design Studio
Chinese Unit 3
Block A picture Changfeng
Changfeng Street Taiyuan
Shanxi Xiaodian 1802, China
Tel: +(0)351 3272666
yuancreate@163.com

332 Jayne Wunder
Jayne Wunder Interior Design
2 Parfitt Close
London NW3 7HW, UK
Tel: +44 (0) 7775 701 441
jaynewunder@gmail.com
www.jaynewunder.com

336 Idmen Liu
Shenzhen Juzhen Mingcui
Design Co., Ltd
Room 2A, Unit 1, Block 6,
Bishuilongting, Longhua
New District, Shenzhen
Guangdong Province, P.R.C.
Mobile: +86 15986695159
Tel: +86 13798559792
vivian_158@163.com
www.idmen.cn

340 Natalia Maslova
3L Décor
Starovolynskaya 15-50
Moscow 119501, Russia
Tel: +7916 116 39 02
maslovanatalia@mail.ru
www.3ldecor.ru

344 Gulia Galeeva
Gulia Galeeva Design
Naberezhnaya Tarasa Shevchenko 1/2
Office 99
121059 Moscow, Russia.
Tel: +7 903 136 93 99
enquiries@guliagaleeva.com
www.guliagaleeva.com

348 Karen Howes
Taylor Howes
49-51 Cheval Place
Knightsbridge
London, SW7 1EW, UK
Tel: +44 207 349 9017
admin@taylorhowes.co.uk
www.taylorhowes.co.uk

352 Michael Del Piero
Michael Del Piero Good Design
428 North Wolcott Chicago
Illinois 60622
Tel:+ 773- 772-3000
info@michaeldelpiero.com
www.michaeldelpiero.com

356 Christopher Dezille
Honky Interior Design & Architecture
Unit 1, Pavement Studios
40-48 Bromells Road
London, SW4 OBG UK
Tel: +44 (0)207 622 7144
Fax: +44 (0) 207 622 7155
info@honky.co.uk
www.honky.co.uk

362 Rob Mills
Rob Mills Architects
10 Grattan Street
Prahran, Melbourne
Australia 3181
Tel: +(03) 9525 2406
Mobile:+ 04 11 102 984
info@robmills.com.au
www.robmills.com.au

366 Steve Leung
Steve Leung Designers Ltd
30/F, Manhattan Place
23 Wang Tai Road
Kowloon Bay
Hong Kong
Tel: +852 2527 1600
Fax: +852 3549 8398
sld@steveleung.com
www.steveleung.com

370 Lucia Valzelli
Dimore di Lucia Valzelli via Gramsci
18, 25121 Brescia
Italy
Tel +39 030 280274
info@dimorestudio.com
www.dimorestudio.com

374 Elisabeth Poppe
Poppe Design
Nobelsgate 23
0268 Oslo, Norway
Tel: +47 900 457 46
post@poppedesign.no
www.poppedesign.no

378 Oleg Klodt and Anna Agapova
Oleg Klodt Architecture & Design
Bolshoy Sukharevskiy pereulok 11/1
127051, Moscow
Russia
Tel: +7 (495) 221 11 58
Mobile: +7 (915) 137 97 96
info@olegklodt.com
www.olegklodt.com

382 Sanjit Singh
Sanjyt Syngh
F-327/1 Lado Sarai
New Delhi – 110030
India
Tel: +91 999 99 75 099
sanjyt@sanjytsyngh.com
www.sanjytsyngh.com

386 Rachel Laxer
London Studio:
St. John's Wood
London, NW8
Tel: +44 (0)207 624 0738
info@rlaxerinteriors.com
www.rlaxerinteriors.com

390 Allison Paladino
Allison Paladino Interior Design
& Collections
11891 US Way 1 Suite 202
North Palm Beach
Fl 33408 USA
Tel: + (561) 741 0165
www.apinteriors.com

394 Angelos Angelopoulos
Angelos Angelopoulos Associates
5 Proairessiou St
116 36 Athens
Greece
Tel: +30 210 756 7191
Fax: +30 210 756 7193
design@angelosangelopoulos.com
www.angelosangelopoulos.com

398 Alessandra Branca
Branca, Inc.
5E. Goethe Street
Chicago, Il 60610 USA
Tel: +312 787 6123 & 1450
info@branca.com
www.branca.com

404 Sophie Ashby
Studio Ashby Ltd
Unit 216 Grand Union Studios
332 Ladbroke Grove
London W10 5AD, UK
Tel: +44 20 3176 2571
info@studioashby.com
www.studioashby.com

410 Arthur Mclaughlin
Mimi Delin
501 Broderick Street
San Francisco
CA, 94117 USA
Tel: 415-673-6746
info@arthurmclaughlin.com
www.arthurmclaughlin.com

414 Prasetio Budhi
Plus Design
JL: Bromo No. 10B
Jakarta 12980
Indonesia
Tel/Fax: +62 21 837 96 131
projects@plus-dsgn.com
www.plus-dsgn.com

420 Claudia Pelizzari
Claudia Pelizzari Interior Design
Corso Matteotti
54 – 25122 Brescia, Italy
Tel: +39 030 290 088
info@pelizzari.com
www.pelizzari.com

424 Geraldine Milsom
Milsom Hotels Ltd
Le Talbooth, Gun Hill
Dedham, Essex
CO7 6HP, UK
Tel: +44 1206 323 150
geraldine@milsomhotels.com
www.milsomhotels.com

428 Elena Uchaeva
Blue Jay Interior Design
Moscow City Business Center
Naberezhnaya Tower, Block C
10 Presnenskaya Nab.
Moscow, 123317
Russia
Tel: +79251782872
Elenauchaeva@yandex.ru
Uchaevaelena@me.com

432 Kunihide Oshinomi
K/O Design Studio
2-28-10 # 105 Jingumae
Shibuya- Ku, Tokyo
Japan 150-0001
Tel: +81 3 5772 2391
Fax: +81 3 5772 2419
kumagai@kodesign.co.jp
www.kodesign.co.jp

438 Anthony Collett &
Andrzej Zarzycki
Collett-Zarzycki Ltd
Fernhead Studios
2B Fernhead Road
London W9 3ET, UK
Tel: +44 208 969 6967
mail@czltd.co.uk
www.collett-zarzycki.com

442 Jumpei Yamagiwa
DESIGN POST
303 Ebisu Flower Home
3-26-3 Higashi
Shibuya-ku, Tokyo
150-0011 Japan
Tel: +81 3 6427 5763
info@designpost.co.jp
www.designpost.co.jp

446 Olga Zubova
Kutuzovsky prospekt 4/2
office XV
1212478 Moscow, Russia
Tel: +7 903 969 47 77
Fax: +7 499 243 57 46
designdecorme@gmail.com

450 Stacey Sibley
Alexander James Interior Design
Berkeley Square House
Berkeley Square
London, W1J 6BD, UK
Tel: +44 (0)20 7887 7604
info@aji.co.uk
www.aji.co.uk

454 Jianguo Liang, Wenqi Cai
Yiqun Wu, Junye Song, Tingyu Liu
Chunkai Nie
Beijing Newsdays Architectural Design
Co., Ltd. China
Jia 10th, Bei San Huan
Zhong Road, West City District
Beijing, P.R. China. P.C:100120
Tel: +86 10 8208 6969
Fax: +86 10 8208 7899
newsdays@newsdaysbj.com
www.beijingnewsdays.com

460 Eric Kuster
Eric Kuster Metropolitan Luxury
Sparrenlaan 11
1272 RN Huizen
The Netherlands
Tel: +31 35 5318773
info@erickuster.com
www.erickuster.com

464 Sophie Paterson
Sophie Paterson Interiors
Surrey
by appointment only
Tel: +44 (0) 1372 462 529
info@sophiepatersoninteriors.com
www.sophiepatersoninteriors.com

468 Bo Li
Cimax Design Engineering
(Hong Kong) Limited/Shenzhen Cimax
Design Company Limited
D Room 12th Floor
Maoye Times Square
Wenxin Road No.2
Nanshan District, Shenzhen City,
Guangdong Province
China
Tel: +86 0755-2644 8677
libodesign@126.com
www.libodesign.com

472 Jenny Weiss & Helen Bygraves
Hill House Interiors Ltd
32-34 Baker Street
Weybridge
Surrey KT13 8AU, UK
Tel: +44 (0) 1932 858 900
design@hillhouseinteriors.com
www.hillhouseinteriors.com

476 Elena Akimova
Elena Akimova Design & Decor
119034, Russia
Moscow
2nd Zachatievski Lane 11, ap.16
Tel: +7 (925) 518 4960
Fax: +43 (676) 942 9210
5261408@gmail.com
elena1218akimova@gmail.com

482 Anna Bilton
Anna Bilton Ltd
6 Passmore Street
London SW1W 8HP, UK
Tel: +44 207 823 6170
info@annabilton.com
www.annabilton.com

488 Juliette Arent & Sarah-Jane Pyke
Arent&Pyke
268 Devonshire Street
Surry Hills
NSW 2010
Australia
Tel: +612 9331 2802
design@arentpyke.com
www.arentpyke.com

492 David T'Kint
Hirsch Bedner Associates (HBA)
Dubai I-Rise Tower
Suite 30-E1, 30th Floor
Al Thanyah First Street
PO Box 390053
Barsha Heights
Dubai UAE
Tel: +971 4 445 8377
Fax: +971 4 445 8376
www.hba.com

498 Nikki Hunt & Andrea Savage
Design Intervention
75E Loewen Road
Tanglin Village
Singapore 248845
Tel: +65 6505 0920
Fax: +65 6468 7418 joann@diid.sg
nikki@diid.sg
www.designintervention.com.sg

502 Fiona Barratt-Campbell
Fiona Barratt Interiors
12 Francis Street
London, SW1P 1QN
Tel: +44 203 262 0320
www.fionabarrattinteriors.com

Editor Martin Waller
Project Executive Annika Bowman
Design by Graphicom Design

teNeues Publishing Group
Kempen
Berlin
London
Munich
New York
Paris

teNeues

Production by Nele Jansen, teNeues Media
Editorial coordination Stephanie Rebel, teNeues Media
Colour separation by SPM Print

First published in 2016 by teNeues Media GmbH & Co. KG, Kempen

teNeues Media GmbH & Co. KG
Am Selder 37, 47906 Kempen, Germany
Phone: +49-(0)2152-916-0
Fax: +49-(0)2152-916-111
e-mail: books@teneues.com

teNeues Publishing Company
7 West 18th Street, New York, NY 10011, USA
Phone: +1-212-627-9090
Fax: +1-212-627-9511

Press department: Andrea Rehn
Phone: +49-(0)2152-916-202
e-mail: arehn@teneues.com

teNeues Publishing UK Ltd.
12 Ferndene Road, London SE24 0AQ, UK
Phone: +44-(0)20-3542-8997

teNeues France S.A.R.L
39, rue des Billets, 18250 Henrichemont, France
Phone: +33-(0)2-4826-9348
Fax: +33-(0)1-7072-3482

www.teneues.com

ISBN 978-3-8327-3425-1
Printed in The Czech Republic

FSC
www.fsc.org

MIX
Papier aus verantwortungsvollen Quellen
Paper from responsible sources
FSC® C005833

Acknowledgments

The author and publisher wish to thank all the owners and designers of the projects featured in this book.

They also thank the following photographers:

Simon Upton, Fritz von der Schulenburg, Melanie Acevedo, James Fennell, Derry Moore, Koen Van Damme, Jan Verlinde, Stijn Rolies, Juan Rodriguez, Frederik Vercruysse, Matthieu Salvaing, Dook, Neil Kirby, Jenny Gorman, Evan Joseph, Liu, Chun-Chieh, Greg Cox, Andreas Von Einsiedel, James Balston, Nick Pope, John Spragg, Viv Yeo/Redcover, Aleksandra Laska, Tubay Yabut, Stephen Busken, David Whittaker, Ian Schemper, Norm Li Architectural Graphics, Arnaud Marthouret, Hill Peppard, Ben Rahn @ A Frame Photography, Dan Couto, Michael Weber, Esto Photography, A Guang, Kate Martin, Jeff McNamara, Giorgio Baroni, Yang Ming, Catherine Gailloud, Hui Wu, Kara Rosenlund, Jared Fowler, Vicente Nebot, Nacása & Partners Inc., Shenzhen LV Feng Photography Ltd, Helenio Barbetta, Wolfgang Stahr, Keita Yamamoto, Serkan Eldeleklioglu, Jonathan Leijonhufvud, Jenni Hare, Kadir Asnaz, Murathan Ozbek, Jane Beiles, Nick Guttridge, Neil Landino, Jia Fang, Gross & Daley, Andrew Boardwin, Dennis Eriksson, Li Zurong, Max Kim-Bee, Manuel Gomes da Costa, Tiago Carvalho, Yunfeng Shi, Werner Straube, Katrina Wittkamp, Trevor Tondro, Michelle Drewes, Bruno Barbosa, Sanda Pagaimo, Paul Craig, Rachael Smith, I.Susa, SEIRYO YAMADA, Anson Smart, Andrew Beasley, Julian Abrams, Mark Williams, Rita Tojal Quintela, Alexander van Berge, Maria Bastos Vasconcelos, Montse Garriga Grau, Francisco Nogueira, Ragnar Hartvig, Peter Bennett, Ray Wong, Frederic Ducout, Lu,Kuo-Chi, Wang,Shih-Yun, Roberta Perrone, Jack Lin, Monsieur Demiere, Faouzi Masrally, El Beit magazine, Yiannis Hadjiaslanis, Pang Xi, Liu Yulin, Mark Williams, Chen Weizhong, Mikhail Stepanov, Tim Beddow, Jon Day, David Garcia, Janet Mesic Mackie, Mark Roper, Earl Carter, Shannon McGrath, Caitlin Mills, Chen Zhong, Elisabeth Aarhus, Andrea Martiradonna, Deepak Aggarwal, Adrian Briscoe, Paul Johnson, Don Freeman, Jessica Glynn Photography, Vangelis Paterakis, Bjorn Wallander, Douglas Friedman, Marco Ricca, Nathan Kirkman, Philip Durrant, Jon Gorrigan, Jacob Elliott, Peter Tjahjadi, Jason Berghdahl, Dan Barber, Shinji Hiraga, Richard Waite, Alexander James, Daisuke Shima, Tse Yin Tat, Karo Avan Dadaev, Tony Mitchell, Jonathan Little, Murray Russell-Langton, Wentao She, Ewoud Rooks, Ray Main, Bo Li, Thierry Cardineau, Laura Kelly, Anna Bilton, Felix Forest, Tom Ferguson, David T'Kint, Eric Laignel, Jo Ann Gamelo-Bernabe.